Pizzas, Pancakes and Pies

Pizzas, Pancakes and Pies

Bloomsbury Books
London

This edition published 1995 by Bloomsbury Books,
an imprint of The Godfrey Cave Group,
42 Bloomsbury Street, London, WC1B 3QJ.

ISBN 1 85471 577 1

Printed and bound in Great Britain

Contents

Pork and Salsify Pie

Serves 6		
Working time: about 1 hour		
Total time: about 4 hours and 15 minutes (includes marinating)		

Calories 340		
Protein 17g		
Cholesterol 65mg		
Total fat 17g		
Saturated fat 8g		
Sodium 310mg		

500 g	lean pork, trimmed and cut into pieces	**1 lb**	**8**	baby onions	**8**
15 cl	dry white wine	**¼ pint**	**125 g**	tomatoes, skinned and chopped	**4 oz**
3	garlic cloves, crushed	**3**	**1 tbsp**	capers, rinsed and chopped	**1 tbsp**
1	small onion, quartered	**1**	**½ tsp**	green peppercorns	**½ tsp**
2	fresh bay leaves and thyme sprigs	**2**	**1 tsp**	arrowroot, mixed with 1 tsp stock or water	**1 tsp**
¼ tsp	salt	**¼ tsp**		**Pastry dough**	
	freshly ground black pepper		**175 g**	plain unbleached flour	**6 oz**
½	lemon, juice only	**½**	**¼ tsp**	salt	**¼ tsp**
250 g	salsify	**8 oz**	**45 g**	unsalted butter, cubed	**1½ oz**
30 cl	unsalted vegetable stock	**½ pint**	**45 g**	white vegetable fat, cubed	**1½ oz**

Put the pork, wine, garlic, onion, bay leaves, thyme, salt and a little pepper in a dish and leave to marinate for 2 hours.

Sift the flour and salt into a large bowl. Rub in the butter and vegetable fat until the mixture has a coarse texture. Sprinkle on water, knead, and press into a ball, then wrap it in plastic film and chill for 15 minutes.

Cook the salsify in boiling water, with lemon juice, until half-tender, then drain.

Put the marinade in a saucepan, simmer for 30 minutes, skimming. Remove the meat,

discard the rest, and add the stock. Return the meat to the pan, add the salsify and baby onions, and simmer for a further 30 minutes.

Preheat the oven to 190°C (375°F or Mark 5). Place a funnel in the centre of a pie dish, add the meat, vegetables, tomatoes, capers and peppercorns. In another pan, bring 30 cl (½ pint) of cooking liquid to the boil with the arrowroot. Simmer to thicken, then pour into the pie dish.

Roll out the dough and place on the dish, leaving a slit for the funnel. Trim and crimp the edges. Bake for 40 minutes and serve hot.

Phyllo Parcels

Serves 4

Working time:
about 45
minutes

Total time:
about 4 hours
(includes
marinating)

Calories
280
Protein
23g
Cholesterol
70mg
Total fat
15g
Saturated fat
4g
Sodium
100mg

500 g	lean pork, trimmed and cubed	**1 lb**	**½ tsp**	salt	**½ tsp**
12.5 cl	red wine	**4 fl oz**	**4**	spinach leaves, stalks removed	**4**
2	garlic cloves, crushed	**2**	**2**	sheets phyllo pastry each about	**2**
1 tsp	fresh thyme leaves, bruised	**1 tsp**		50 by 28 cm (20 by 11 inches)	
1 tsp	mixed peppercorns, crushed	**1 tsp**	**2 tbsp**	safflower oil	**2 tbsp**
15 g	dried ceps	**½ oz**	**4 tsp**	redcurrant jelly	**4 tsp**

Put the pork cubes, wine, garlic, thyme leaves and crushed peppercorns in a dish. Cover and leave to marinate for at least 3 hours. Soak the ceps in warm water for 20 minutes.

Drain the meat and pat the cubes dry. Reserve the unabsorbed marinade. Drain the ceps, rinse, then dry and chop them roughly.

Gently sauté the meat in a dry frying pan, turning regularly, until the cubes are browned and cooked through. Stir in the mushrooms, the reserved marinade and the salt. Reduce the liquid, then remove the pan from the heat.

Plunge the spinach leaves into boiling water, drain, refresh, and lay out to dry.

Preheat the oven to 190°C (375°F or Mark 5).

Cut each phyllo sheet lengthwise in half to make four long strips. Position one strip with a short side towards you and brush lightly with oil. Place one spinach leaf at the end of the strip then put a quarter of the meat mixture in a pile on the spinach. Lift one corner of the strip and fold it over the filling so that the corner meets the opposite long side, then fold the package towards the far end of the strip. Continue folding alternately across and up the strip until you reach the far end; any short band of phyllo remaining at the far end may be trimmed off. Repeat with the other strips and the rest of the spinach and meat.

Brush the packages lightly with the remaining oil and place them on a non-stick baking sheet. Bake in the oven for 20 minutes, turning once, until they are golden and crisp. Serve hot, with a spoonful of redcurrant jelly.

Picnic Slice

Serves 10

Working time:
about 35
minutes

Total time:
about 3 hours
(includes
chilling)

Calories
290
Protein
13g
Cholesterol
70mg
Total fat
15g
Saturated fat
6g
Sodium
275mg

350 g	lean pork, minced	**12 oz**
125 g	brown rice	**4 oz**
1	bunch spring onions, chopped	**1**
2	eggs, hard-boiled and chopped	**2**
2 tbsp	chopped fresh tarragon	**2 tbsp**
2 tbsp	capers, rinsed and drained	**2 tbsp**
8	green olives, stoned and chopped	**8**

50 g	anchovy fillets, chopped	**1¾ oz**
	Flaky pastry	
200 g	plain flour	**7 oz**
½ tsp	salt	**½ tsp**
60 g	unsalted butter, slightly softened	**2 oz**
60 g	hard white vegetable fat	**2 oz**

Sift the flour and salt into a bowl. Rub in the butter and vegetable fat until the mixture resembles breadcrumbs. Add enough water to make it cohere. Make a ball, wrap it with film and place in the refrigerator for 30 minutes.

On a floured board, roll the dough into a rectangle about three times as long as it is wide. With a short side towards you, dot the top two thirds of the rectangle with another quarter of the fat, fold the bottom third of the rectangle over the centre and the top third over that, and chill for 30 minutes. Roll out, dot with fat, fold and chill in the same way two more times, then roll out the dough to make the final folds cohere. Wrap in plastic film and refrigerate.

Cook the rice, rinse, and leave to cool.

Brown the pork, stir in the spring onions and cook for another 2 minutes.

Preheat the oven to 220°C (425°F or Mark 7). Divide the pastry dough in two. Roll each piece into a thin sheet about 30 by 25 cm (12 by 10 inches) and place these on non-stick baking sheets. Spread the rice down the centre of each sheet, leaving bare pastry on each side of the filling. Lay the meat mixture, the eggs, tarragon, capers, olives and anchovies on top.

Brush the edges of the pastry with water, then bring the side flaps up and fold one over the other. Crimp the joints, turn over, and cut slits in the pastry top to let the steam escape.

Bake until golden-brown then lower the heat and cook for another 20 minutes.

Spicy Shrimp Griddle Cakes

Serves 6

Working (and total) time about 30 minutes

Calories
245
Protein
12g
Cholesterol
70mg
Total fat
6g
Saturated fat
3g
Sodium
295mg

150 g	cornmeal	**5 oz**
75 g	plain flour	**2¼ oz**
2 tsp	baking powder	**2 tsp**
1 tsp	dried thyme	**1 tsp**
1 tsp	dried oregano	**1 tsp**
¼ tsp	salt	**¼ tsp**
¼ tsp	ground white pepper	**¼ tsp**
¼ tsp	cayenne pepper	**¼ tsp**
3	large garlic cloves, chopped	**3**

1	spring onion, finely chopped	**1**
1	small sweet red pepper, seeded, deribbed and finely chopped	**1**
30 g	unsalted butter, melted	**1 oz**
40 cl	semi-skimmed milk	**13 fl oz**
250 g	cooked, peeled shrimps	**8 oz**
1	lemon, cut into wedges, for garnish	**1**
	several parsley sprigs for garnish	

Combine the cornmeal, flour, baking powder, thyme, oregano, salt, white pepper and cayenne pepper in a bowl. Stir in the garlic, spring onion and red pepper. Whisk in the melted butter and the milk, mixing until all the ingredients are just blended. Stir in the shrimps.

Heat a large griddle or frying pan over medium heat until a few drops of cold water dance when sprinkled on the surface. Drop the batter a generous tablespoon at a time on to the griddle and use the back of the spoon to spread the batter into rounds. Cook the griddle cakes until they are covered with bubbles and the undersides are golden—1 to 3 minutes. Flip and cook until the second sides are lightly browned—about 1 minute more. Transfer the griddle cakes to a platter and keep them warm while you cook the remaining batter. Serve the griddle cakes piping hot, garnished with the lemon wedges and parsley sprigs.

Tropical Puffed Pancake

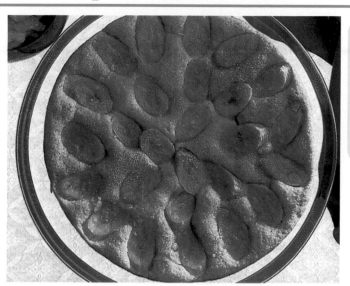

	Serves 4
	Working time: about 30 minutes
	Total time: about 45 minutes

Calories	350
Protein	9g
Cholesterol	140mg
Total fat	8g
Saturated fat	2g
Sodium	265mg

3 tbsp	caster sugar	3 tbsp
¼ tsp	ground cinnamon	¼ tsp
35 g	plain flour	1¼ oz
30 g	wholemeal flour	1 oz
½ tsp	baking powder	½ tsp
¼ tsp	salt	¼ tsp
2	eggs, separated, plus 1 egg white	2
1 tbsp	light or dark rum	1 tbsp
1 tbsp	safflower oil	1 tbsp

1	lemon, grated rind only	1
17.5 cl	semi-skimmed milk	6 fl oz
2	bananas, sliced diagonally	2
	Rum-pineapple topping	
300 g	pineapple flesh, chopped	10 oz
2 tbsp	dark brown sugar	2 tbsp
2 tbsp	raisins	2 tbsp
1	lemon, juice only	1
2 tbsp	light or dark rum	2 tbsp

To make the rum-pineapple topping, put the pineapple into a heavy saucepan and stir in the brown sugar, raisins and lemon juice. Bring the mixture to the boil, then reduce the heat, and simmer for 5 minutes. Remove from the heat and stir in the rum. Keep the topping warm while you prepare the puffed pancake.

In a small bowl, mix 2 tablespoons of the caster sugar with the cinnamon and set aside. Preheat the oven to 220°C (425°F or Mark 7).

Sift the two flours, the baking powder, the salt and the remaining caster sugar into a bowl. In a separate bowl, whisk the egg yolks with

the rum and the oil; stir in the lemon rind and the milk. Whisk the flour mixture into the milk mixture to make a smooth, thin batter.

Beat the egg whites until they form soft peaks. Stir half of the egg whites into the batter and then fold in the remaining egg whites.

Ladle the batter into a warmed casserole dish. Cook the pancake for 2 minutes; top it with the sliced bananas and sprinkle it with the cinnamon sugar. Bake the until it puffs up and is golden-brown—10 to 12 minutes.

Cut the pancake into four wedges and serve it immediately with the rum-pineapple topping.

Potato Griddle Cakes with Apple-Mustard Compote

Serves 8			Calories 205
Working time: about 45 minutes			Protein 3g
Total time: about 1 hour and 10 minutes			Cholesterol 40mg
			Total fat 4g
			Saturated fat 2g
			Sodium 160mg

1	potato, peeled and diced	1	6	firm apples, peeled, cored,	6
1	egg, separated, plus 1 egg white	1		quartered, and cut into eighths	
1 tsp	caster sugar	1 tsp	6 tbsp	sugar	6 tbsp
¼ tsp	salt	¼ tsp	30 g	unsalted butter	1 oz
⅛ tsp	grated nutmeg	⅛ tsp	40 g	sultanas	1¼ oz
75 g	plain flour	2½ oz	1	lemon, grated rind and juice	1
	Apple-mustard compote		½ tsp	ground cinnamon	½ tsp
6 tbsp	unsweetened apple juice	6 tbsp	2 tbsp	grainy mustard	2 tbsp

Boil the potato until soft—10 to 15 minutes.

Put the apples, sugar, apple juice, butter, sultanas, lemon rind and lemon juice into a heavy frying pan over medium-high heat. Cook the mixture, stirring frequently, until the apples are tender—about 5 minutes. Stir in the cinnamon and mustard, and keep warm.

Drain the cooked potato, reserving ¼ litre (8 fl oz) of the cooking liquid. Put in a bowl and mash until smooth. Stir in the reserved cooking liquid and let it cool. Stir in the egg yolk, sugar, salt and nutmeg. Sift in the flour and stir the mixture just until it is blended.

Put the egg whites into a bowl and beat them until they form soft peaks. Stir about a quarter of the egg whites into the potato mixture and then gently fold in the remaining egg whites.

Heat a large frying pan over medium heat and spoon on about 4 tablespoons of the batter at a time. Use the back of the spoon to spread the batter into rounds. Cook the griddle cakes until they are covered with bubbles and the undersides are golden—1 to 3 minutes. Flip and cook them until the second sides are lightly browned. Transfer the cakes to a platter and keep them warm while you cook the remaining batter. Serve the griddle cakes immediately with the apple-mustard compote.

Cornmeal Buttermilk Pancakes

Serves 6

Working
(and total)
time: about
20 minutes

Calories
285
Protein
8g
Cholesterol
95mg
Total fat
7g
Saturated fat
1g
Sodium
245mg

175 g	plain flour	**6 oz**	**125 g**	cornmeal	**4 oz**
3 tbsp	caster sugar	**3 tbsp**	**2**	eggs	**2**
½ tsp	bicarbonate of soda	**½ tsp**	**35 cl**	buttermilk	**12 fl oz**
¼ tsp	salt	**¼ tsp**	**2 tbsp**	safflower oil	**2 tbsp**

Sift the flour, sugar, bicarbonate of soda and salt into a mixing bowl; stir in the cornmeal. In another bowl, whisk together the eggs, buttermilk and oil.

Pour the buttermilk mixture into the dry ingredients and whisk them quickly together until they are just blended; do not overmix.

Heat a large griddle or frying pan over medium heat until a few drops of cold water dance when sprinkled on the surface. Drop 2 tablespoons of the batter on to the hot griddle or pan, and use the back of the spoon to spread the batter into a round. Fill the pan with pancakes; cook them until the tops are covered with bubbles and the undersides are golden— 1 to 2 minutes. Flip the pancakes over and cook them until the second sides are lightly browned—about 1 minute more. Transfer the pancakes to a platter and keep them warm while you cook the remaining batter.

Serve the pancakes immediately, with a topping of your choice.

Rye Griddle Cakes

Serves 8

Working
(and total)
time: about
30 minutes

Calories
155
Protein
10g
Cholesterol
80mg
Total fat
3g
Saturated fat
1g
Sodium
315mg

2	eggs, plus 2 egg whites	**2**
15 cl	semi-skimmed milk	**¼ pint**
2	large spring onions, trimmed and chopped	**2**
¼ tsp	salt	**¼ tsp**
	freshly ground black pepper	

250 g	fresh dark rye breadcrumbs	**8 oz**
	Accompaniments	
175 g	yogurt cheese	**6 oz**
1 tbsp	red lumpfish caviare	**1 tbsp**
1	spring onion, sliced diagonally	**1**
1	lemon, thinly sliced (optional)	**1**

Whisk together the eggs, egg whites, milk, finely chopped spring onions, salt and a generous grinding of pepper in a bowl. Stir in the breadcrumbs to make a smooth mixture.

Heat a large griddle or frying pan over medium heat until a few drops of water dance when sprinkled on the surface. Drop the batter 1 generous tablespoon at a time on to the griddle or pan, and use the back of the spoon to spread the batter into ovals. Cook the griddle cakes until they are covered with bubbles—1 to 3 minutes. Turn each cake and cook the second side for 1 minute more. Transfer the cakes to a platter and keep them warm while you cook the remaining batter.

Accompany each serving with a dollop of yogurt cheese topped with some caviare and sliced spring onion. Garnish with lemon.

Griddle Cheesecakes with Cranberry Sauce

450 g	low-fat cottage cheese	**15 oz**
2	eggs	**2**
45 g	caster sugar	**$1\frac{1}{2}$ oz**
150 g	plain flour	**5 oz**
1 tsp	baking powder	**1 tsp**
1	lemon, grated rind only	**1**

	Cranberry sauce	
100 g	sugar	**$3\frac{1}{2}$ oz**
1 tbsp	cornflour	**1 tbsp**
35 cl	fresh orange juice	**12 fl oz**
200 g	fresh or frozen cranberries	**7 oz**

To make the cranberry sauce, combine the sugar and cornflour in a heavy saucepan. Pour in the orange juice, stirring continuously. Add the cranberries and bring the mixture to the boil over medium heat, stirring constantly. Reduce the heat and simmer until all the cranberries have burst—about 15 minutes. Purée the mixture in a blender and then pass it through a sieve into a bowl. Set the sauce aside in a warm place.

Rinse out the blender and purée the cottage cheese in it. Add the eggs and blend them into the purée. Transfer the mixture to a bowl and stir in the sugar, flour and baking powder, beating just long enough to produce a smooth batter. Stir the lemon rind into the batter.

Heat a large griddle or frying pan over medium heat. Drop a generous tablespoon of the batter on to the hot griddle or pan, and use the back of the spoon to spread the batter to a thickness of 5 mm ($\frac{1}{4}$ inch). Form several more batter rounds in the same way, then cook the griddle cheesecakes until they are covered with bubbles and the undersides are golden— about 3 minutes. Flip the cheesecakes and cook them until the second sides are lightly browned—about 1 minute more. Transfer the cheesecakes to a platter and keep them warm while you cook the remaining batter.

Serve the griddle cheesecakes accompanied by the cranberry sauce.

Paprika Blintzes

Serves 4

Working time:
about 50
minutes

Total time:
about 1 hour
and 30
minutes

Calories
225
Protein
14g
Cholesterol
80mg
Total fat
10g
Saturated fat
3g
Sodium
420mg

75 g	plain flour	2½ oz
¼ tsp	salt	⅛ tsp
1½ tsp	paprika	1½ tsp
1	egg	1
17.5 cl	semi-skimmed milk	6 fl oz
1 tbsp	virgin olive oil	1 tbsp
1½ tsp	fresh thyme	1½ tsp
¼ tsp	safflower oil	¼ tsp

Cheese and spring onion filling

1½ tsp	virgin olive oil	1½ tsp
1	garlic clove, finely chopped	1
2	bunches spring onions, chopped	2
1½ tsp	fresh thyme	1½ tsp
	freshly ground black pepper	
⅛ tsp	salt	⅛ tsp
175 g	low-fat cottage cheese	175 g
12.5 cl	plain low-fat yogurt	4 fl oz
2 tbsp	grated Parmesan cheese	2 tbsp

To make the crêpes, sift the flour, salt and paprika into a bowl. Make a well in the centre, then add the egg, milk, olive oil and thyme. Whisk the mixture, gradually incorporating the flour. Cover and let it stand for 1 hour.

Heat the olive oil in a heavy-bottomed saucepan over medium-high heat. Add the garlic, spring onions, thyme, some pepper and the salt. Cook, stirring frequently, until the spring onions are soft. Transfer to a bowl.

Put the cottage cheese, yogurt and Parmesan cheese into a blender. Add the puréed mixture to the spring onions. Stir well, then set aside.

Heat, and evenly oil, the crêpe pan. Ladle on about 3 tablespoons of the batter and swirl the pan to get an even layer. Cook until the bottom is browned. Turn over and cook. Repeat the process to form eight crêpes in all.

Preheat the oven to 200°C (400°F or Mark 6). Spoon about 4 tablespoons of the cheese and spring onion mixture on to each crêpe near its edge. Fold in to form an envelope round the filling. Bake each of the crêpes until they are crisp and lightly browned. Serve immediately.

Broccoli and Ricotta Pie

Serves 6 as
a main dish

Working
time: about
1 hour

Total time:
about 2
hours

Calories
325

Protein
17g

Cholesterol
65mg

Total fat
8g

Saturated fat
3g

Sodium
285mg

1 tbsp	easy-blend dried yeast	1 tbsp	17.5 cl	semi-skimmed milk	6 fl oz
375 g	strong plain flour	13 oz		freshly ground black pepper	
$\frac{1}{4}$ tsp	salt	$\frac{1}{4}$ tsp	$\frac{1}{8}$ tsp	grated nutmeg	$\frac{1}{8}$ tsp
1 tbsp	virgin olive oil	1 tbsp	30 g	mild back bacon, chopped	1 oz
250 g	onion, chopped	8 oz	1 tbsp	cornmeal	1 tbsp
$\frac{1}{2}$ tsp	caraway seeds	$\frac{1}{2}$ tsp	350 g	broccoli florets, blanched in	12 oz
1	egg, plus 2 egg whites	1		boiling water for 1 minute	
175 g	low-fat ricotta cheese	6 oz	2 tbsp	grated Parmesan cheese	2 tbsp

Mix the yeast with 140 g (5 oz) of the flour and $\frac{1}{8}$ teaspoon of the salt. Pour hot water into the flour mixture and stir vigorously. Stir in 1 teaspoon of the oil and another 140 g (5 oz) of the flour. Knead until smooth and elastic—about 10 minutes. Transfer to an oiled bowl, turn once to coat it with oil, and cover. Set in a warm place and let the dough rise until it has doubled in volume—about 30 minutes.

Gently fry the onion and the caraway seeds, until the onion is lightly browned. Set aside.

Whisk the egg and the egg whites in a large bowl. Add the ricotta, milk, the remaining salt, some black pepper, the nutmeg and the bacon.

Stir in half of the onion mixture and set aside.

Preheat the oven to 200°C (400°F or Mark 6). After the dough has finished rising, knock it back and knead in the remaining onion mixture.

Sprinkle a shallow casserole with the cornmeal. Add the dough and form a 5 cm (2 inch) rim. Allow to stand for 10 minutes.

Partially bake the dough for 10 minutes. Remove from the oven and pour in the ricotta egg mixture. Place the broccoli florets, bud sides up, in the filling, then sprinkle on the Parmesan. Return to the oven and bake until the top is lightly browned. Let stand for 10 minutes serving.

Cornmeal Griddle Cakes

125 g	cornmeal	4 oz	12.5 cl	semi-skimmed milk	4 fl oz
1 tsp	sugar	1 tsp	1	egg lightly beaten	1
¼ tsp	salt	¼ tsp			

Combine the cornmeal, sugar and salt. Pour in ¼ litre (8 fl oz) of boiling water all at once and stir until the ingredients are all well blended. Let the mixture stand for 2 minutes.

In a small bowl, whisk together the milk and egg. Pour this mixture into the bowl containing the cornmeal mixture and stir the batter until it is smooth.

Heat a large, non-stick griddle or frying pan over medium-high heat until a few drops of cold water dance when sprinkled on the surface. Drop the batter, 2 tablespoons at a time, on to the hot surface, then use the back of the spoon to spread the batter into 10 cm (4 inch) rounds. Cook the griddle cakes until the surfaces are covered with bubbles and the undersides are browned—about 2 minutes. Turn the cakes over and cook them until the other sides are browned—about 1 minute more.

Transfer the griddle cakes to a serving plate and keep them warm while you cook the remaining batter. Serve the griddle cakes warm.

Pear Pizza

Serves 8

Working time:
about 45
minutes

Total time:
about 1 hour
and 45
minutes

Calories
210
Protein
4g
Cholesterol
4mg
Total fat
2g
Saturated fat
1g
Sodium
35mg

240 g	strong plain flour	**8 ¼ oz**	
100 g	caster sugar	**3 ½ oz**	
1 tsp	grated lemon rind	**1 tsp**	
⅛ tsp	salt	**⅛ tsp**	
1 tbsp	easy-blend dried yeast	**1 tbsp**	
15 g	unsalted butter	**½ oz**	

6 tbsp	currants or raisins, chopped	**6 tbsp**
600 g	pears, quartered, cored, peeled and thinly sliced	**1¼ lb**
2 tbsp	fresh lemon juice	**2 tbsp**
2 tbsp	cornmeal	**2 tbsp**

Combine 75 g (2½ oz) of the flour, 2 tablespoons of the sugar, the lemon rind, salt and yeast. In a small saucepan, heat 17.5 cl (6 fl oz) of water until it is hot to the touch, then pour it into the mixture, and mix. Gradually stir in enough of the remaining flour to make a dough that can be formed into a ball. Knead until it is smooth and elastic—5 to 10 minutes. Put the dough into a large, lightly oiled bowl and coat it with the oil. Cover with a damp towel and place in a warm place. Let it rise until it has doubled in bulk—30 to 45 minutes.

In the meantime, heat the butter in a large, heavy frying pan over medium-high heat. Add the currants or raisins and the pears, and cook, stirring frequently, for 5 minutes. Add the

lemon juice and all but 1 tablespoon of the remaining sugar; continue cooking the mixture until the pears are soft and the sugar begins to brown—about 5 minutes more.

Preheat the oven to 230°C (450°F or Mark 8). Lightly oil a baking sheet and sprinkle it with the cornmeal. When the dough has risen, return it to the floured surface and knead it for 1 minute. Flatten it into a 25 cm (10 inch) round and transfer it to the baking sheet.

Spread the pear topping over the dough, leaving a border of dough all round. Sprinkle the reserved tablespoon of sugar over the pear topping, then bake until the crust is well browned. Remove from the oven and let stand for 5 minutes before slicing and serving.

Cheese Pinwheels

Makes 8
pinwheels

Working time:
about 30
minutes

Total time:
about 45
minutes

Per pinwheel:
Calories
210
Protein
7g
Cholesterol
2mg
Total fat
4g
Saturated fat
1g
Sodium
270mg

225 g	plain flour	**7½ oz**
90 g	wholemeal flour	**3 oz**
3 tbsp	caster sugar	**3 tbsp**
2 tsp	baking powder	**2 tsp**
½ tsp	bicarbonate of soda	**½ tsp**
⅛ tsp	salt	**⅛ tsp**
¼ tsp	ground cinnamon	**¼ tsp**
¼ litre	plain low-fat yogurt	**8 fl oz**

2 tbsp	safflower oil	**2 tbsp**
30 g	icing sugar, sifted	**1 oz**
2 tsp	semi-skimmed milk	**2 tsp**
	Cheese and lemon filling	
125 g	low-fat cottage cheese	**4 oz**
2 tsp	caster sugar	**2 tsp**
1	lemon, grated rind only	**1**

To make the filling, purée the cottage cheese until no trace of curd remains. Add the 2 teaspoons of caster sugar and the lemon rind; process the mixture until the ingredients are blended. Set aside.

Preheat the oven to 200°C (400°F or Mark 6); lightly oil a baking sheet. Combine the flours, the 3 tablespoons of caster sugar, the baking powder, bicarbonate of soda, salt and cinnamon in a large bowl. In a smaller bowl, whisk together the yogurt and the oil; stir this mixture into the dry ingredients. Turn the dough on to a floured surface and knead it to fully incorporate the ingredients.

Divide the dough in half. Roll out one half of the dough and trim it into a 20 cm (8 inch) square, then cut the square into four 10 cm (4 inch) squares. Form a pinwheel, using 1 tablespoon of the cheese filling. With a spatula, transfer the pinwheel to the baking sheet. Repeat the procedure with the remaining dough.

Bake the pinwheels until they are golden-brown—10 to 12 minutes. Just before the pastries are done, mix the icing sugar and the milk in a small bowl. Dribble or brush the sugar glaze over the pinwheels as soon as they are removed from the oven. Serve hot.

Pork and Spinach Pie

Serves 6 as
a main course

Working time:
about 30
minutes

Total time:
about 1 hour

Calories
300

Protein
22g

Cholesterol
85mg

Total fat
11g

Saturated fat
4g

Sodium
570mg

300 g	frozen chopped spinach	**10 oz**
250 g	pork fillet, trimmed and chopped	**8 oz**
1 tsp	fennel seeds	**1 tsp**
2	garlic cloves, finely chopped	**2**
1 tsp	ground coriander	**1 tsp**
⅛ tsp	salt	**⅛ tsp**
1 tbsp	virgin olive oil	**1 tbsp**

½ tsp	dried hot red pepper flakes	**½ tsp**
60 cl	butter milk	**1 pint**
1	egg, plus 1 egg white	**1**
1	loaf French bread, cut into 1 cm (½ inch) slices	**1**
60 g	Parmesan cheese, freshly grated	**2 oz**

Microwave the spinach on high for 2½ minutes to defrost. Set aside.

Mix together the pork, fennel seeds, garlic, coriander, salt, ½ tablespoon of oil and ¼ teaspoon of pepper flakes. In another bowl, mix the buttermilk, egg and egg white, the remaining oil and the remaining pepper flakes.

Spread the bread slices in a single layer on the bottom of a shallow baking tray. Pour on all but 4 tablespoons of the buttermilk mixture, then turn the slices. Let the bread stand, turning the slices frequently until they have absorbed nearly all the liquid—about 15 minutes.

Microwave the pork mixture on high for 1½ minutes, stirring the mixture once at midpoint.

Remove the spinach from the package and squeeze to remove as much liquid as possible. Stir the spinach into the pork mixture, along with the reserved 4 tablespoons of the buttermilk mixture and about half the cheese.

Spoon about a quarter of the pork mixture into a 28 cm (11 inch) glass pie plate. Arrange half of the bread slices in a close-fitting layer on top of the pork. Repeat and pour on any remaining buttermilk mixture. Cover the dish.

Microwave on medium for 4 minutes. Rotate and cook for another 4 minutes. Uncover and scatter the remaining cheese over the top. Cook the dish 8 minutes more. Let the dish stand for at least 5 minutes before serving it.

Cheddar and Vegetable Phyllo Roll

Serves 6 as a side dish

Working time: about 40 minutes

Total time: about 1 hour and 15 minutes

Calories 145
Protein 6g
Cholesterol 7mg
Total fat 6g
Saturated fat 2g
Sodium 160mg

500 g	broccoli florets	**1 lb**
4 tsp	safflower oil	**4 tsp**
1	shallot, finely chopped	**1**
2	large courgettes, grated	**2**
6 tbsp	dry vermouth	**6 tbsp**
2 tbsp	plain flour	**2 tbsp**
12.5 cl	semi-skimmed milk	**4 fl oz**
30 g	Cheddar cheese, grated	**1 oz**
⅛ tsp	salt	**⅛ tsp**
4	sheets phyllo dough	**4**

Pour enough water into a saucepan to fill it 2.5 cm (1 inch) deep. Set a vegetable steamer in the pan and bring the water to the boil. Put the broccoli into the steamer, cover the pan tightly, and steam the broccoli until it is tender—about 7 minutes. When the broccoli has cooled, chop it coarsely and set it aside.

Preheat the oven to 220°C (425°F or Mark 7). Heat 2 teaspoons of the oil in a large non-stick frying pan over medium-high heat. Add the shallot and sauté it until it is translucent—about 2 minutes. Add the courgette and cook it, stirring continuously, until it is tender—about 2 minutes more. Reduce the heat to medium, add the broccoli and vermouth to the vegetables, and cook them until the vermouth has evaporated—approximately 5 minutes.

Stir the flour into the vegetables. Add the milk and continue cooking the mixture, stirring continuously, until the liquid comes to the boil. Add the cheese and salt and set the pan aside.

Place the phyllo sheets, stacked on top of each other, on a work surface. Spoon the cooled vegetable mixture lengthwise down the centre of the top sheet. Fold a long side of the stack of sheets over the filling and brush the edge lightly with some of the oil. Fold the other long side over to cover the filling.

Brush both ends with about 1 teaspoon of the remaining oil. Fold up the ends to enclose the filling. Turn the phyllo roll seam side down and set it on a baking sheet. Brush the top surface with the remaining oil and bake until the phyllo is crisp—approximately 20 minutes.

Individual Tomato Pizzas

Serves 4

Working time:
about 45
minutes

Total time:
about 3 hours
(includes
rising and
cooling)

Calories
345
Protein
10g
Cholesterol
55mg
Total fat
9g
Saturated fat
3g
Sodium
135mg

250 g	strong white flour	**8 oz**	**1 tbsp**	tomato paste		**1 tbsp**
¼ tsp	salt	**¼ tsp**	**1 tbsp**	chopped fresh basil		**1 tbsp**
15 g	unsalted butter	**½ oz**	**1 tsp**	chopped fresh marjoram		**1 tsp**
1 tsp	easy-blend dried yeast	**1 tsp**	**90 g**	button mushrooms, sliced		**3 oz**
1 tbsp	safflower oil	**1 tbsp**		freshly ground black pepper		
250 g	onions, thinly sliced	**8 oz**	**¼**	green pepper, blanched for 2 minutes		**¼**
2	garlic cloves, crushed	**2**	**4**	quail's eggs, hard boiled, sliced		**4**
500 g	tomatoes, skinned and sliced	**1 lb**	**1**	large black olive, stoned and sliced		**1**

Sift the flour and ¼ teaspoon of the salt into a bowl, and rub in the butter. Sprinkle on the dried yeast, and mix thoroughly. Add sufficient warm water to form a pliable dough and knead it until it is smooth. Put the dough into a large, oiled polythene bag, and fold over the top. Set aside in a warm place to rise for about 1 hour.

Heat the oil in a heavy saucepan, and fry the onions and garlic gently until the onions are soft. Add the tomatoes and tomato paste, and continue cooking for another 5 to 8 minutes. Add the herbs, the mushrooms, the remaining salt and some pepper, and cook until the mushrooms are soft. Set aside.

Lightly grease four flan tins, and place them on a baking sheet. Knock back the dough, and knead it until smooth. Quarter the dough, keeping the unrolled dough covered with plastic film while you are working. Roll out each piece of dough to a thickness of about 5 mm (¼ inch). Line each of the tins with a portion and spread on the cooled tomato mixture. Set aside to rise in a warm place, uncovered, for 10 to 15 minutes, until they are puffy. Preheat the oven to 220°C (425°F or Mark 7).

Bake until the edges of the pizza are lightly browned. Garnish with the green pepper, olive slivers and quaill's eggs.

Baked Vegetable Samosas

Makes 8
samosas

Working time:
about 1 hour

Total time:
about 1 hour
and 25
minutes

Per samosa:
Calories
170
Protein
5g
Cholesterol
30mg
Total fat
7g
Saturated fat
2g
Sodium
70mg

1	potato, peeled and quartered	1
1	small carrot, quartered lengthwise	1
1 tsp	safflower oil	1 tsp
2 tsp	fresh lemon juice	2 tsp
1	leek, trimmed and shredded	1
45 g	frozen peas	1½ oz
1	green chili pepper, chopped	1
¾ tsp	cumin seeds	¾ tsp
2 tsp	ground turmeric	2 tsp
¾ tsp	ground coriander	¾ tsp
1	small egg, beaten, for glazing	1
1 tbsp	poppy seeds	1 tbsp
	Shortcrust pastry	
140 g	plain flour	4½ oz
45 g	brown flour	1½ oz
45 g	polyunsaturated margarine	1½ oz
3½ tbsp	skimmed milk	3½ tbsp

Boil the potato and carrot for 10 minutes. Drain, then chop them and set them aside. Put the oil, lemon juice, leek, peas, chili pepper. cumin seeds, turmeric and coriander in a small saucepan. Add 1 tablespoon of water and cook for 3 minutes, stirring frequently. Stir in the potato and carrot and leave to cool.

For the pastry, put the plain flour and brown flour in a mixing bowl and rub in the margarine until the mixture resembles fine breadcrumbs. Add the milk and mix it in to form a dough. Form into a ball and knead it until smooth. Divide into four. Form each portion into a ball,

then roll out each ball into an 18 cm (7 inch) round. Trim the rounds, then cut each in half.

Preheat the oven to 190°C (375°F or Mark 5). Lightly grease a baking sheet. Divide the vegetable mixture evenly among the semicircles of dough, mounding it on one half, leaving a border free of filling. Lightly dampen the edges of each semicircle with water, then fold the dough over. Decorate each rounded edge with the tip of a knife.

Brush the samosas lightly with the beaten egg and sprinkle on poppy seeds. Bake until golden-brown. Cool on a wire rack, then serve.

Rump Steak Pasties

Serves 4

Working time:
about 50
minutes

Total time:
about 2 hours
and 50 minutes
(includes
cooling)

Calories
365
Protein
15g
Cholesterol
20mg
Total fat
16g
Saturated fat
4g
Sodium
230mg

1 tsp	virgin olive oil	1 tsp
125 g	potatoes, peeled and diced	4 oz
90 g	carrots, diced	3 oz
90 g	swede, peeled and diced	3 oz
1	onion, finely chopped	1
125 g	rump steak, trimmed and cut into 1 cm ($\frac{1}{2}$ inch) dice	4 oz
1 tbsp	chopped fresh oregano	1 tbsp

3 tbsp	unsalted veal stock or water	3 tbsp
$\frac{1}{8}$ tsp	salt	$\frac{1}{8}$ tsp
	freshly ground black pepper	
1	egg white, beaten	1
	Shortcrust pastry	
175 g	plain flour	6 oz
$\frac{1}{8}$ tsp	salt	$\frac{1}{8}$ tsp
60 g	polyunsaturated margarine	2 oz

Heat the olive oil in a large frying pan over medium heat. Add the potatoes, carrots, swede and onion, and cook until they just begin to soften. Remove from the heat and allow to cool.

To make the pastry, sift the flour and salt into a bowl and rub in the margarine until the mixture resembles fine breadcrumbs. Make a well in the centre and pour in 3 tablespoons of water. Mix the ingredients together to form a firm dough. Gather into a ball and knead it on a lightly floured surface until smooth. Divide into four equal pieces. Roll out each piece to a round, about 15 cm (6 inches) in diameter, and trim the edges.

Add the diced rump steak to the cooled vegetables, then stir in the oregano, veal stock, salt, and some black pepper. Place a quarter of the mixture in the centre of each pastry round, and brush the edges with the beaten egg white. Taking one round at a time, carefully bring two opposite sides together until they meet in the centre of the filling. Press the edges together and crimp the joined edges.

Refrigerate the pasties for .20 minutes. Preheat the oven to 220°C (425°F or Mark 7).

Brush each pasty with the remaining beaten egg white, then bake for 25 to 30 minutes, or until they are golden-brown.

Courgette and Camembert Quiche

Serves 8

Working time:
about 30
minutes

Total time:
about 1 hour
and 35
minutes

Calories
250
Protein
8g
Cholesterol
70mg
Total fat
13g
Saturated fat
3g
Sodium
3mg

600 g	courgettes, sliced	**1¼ lb**	**2**	eggs, beaten		**2**
1 tsp	polyunsaturated margarine	**1 tsp**	**⅛ tsp**	salt		**⅛ tsp**
1	onion, finely chopped	**1**		freshly ground black pepper		
1½ tbsp	chopped fresh basil	**1½ tbsp**		**Shortcrust pastry**		
140 g	Camembert, rind removed,	**4½ oz**	**200 g**	plain flour		**7 oz**
	cut into pieces		**⅛ tsp**	salt		**⅛ tsp**
30 cl	skimmed milk	**½ pint**	**90 g**	polyunsaturated margarine		**3 oz**

Preheat the oven to 180°C (350°F or Mark 4). Place the sliced courgettes in a lightly oiled baking dish, cover with foil and bake until they are tender—about 20 minutes.

Meanwhile, sift the flour and salt for the pastry into a large bowl, then rub in the chilled margarine until the mixture resembles fine breadcrumbs. Using a round-bladed knife, stir in 3 to 4 tablespoons of water to make a firm dough. Knead it until it is smooth. Roll out the dough and use it to line a 2.5 cm (1 inch) deep 22 cm (9 inch) flan dish. Prick the base and sides with a fork and chill for 20 minutes.

Increase the oven temperature to 200°C (400°F or Mark 6). Bake the pastry case for 15

minutes, then remove it from the oven and set it aside. Reduce the oven temperature to 180°C (350°F or Mark 4).

Melt the margarine in a heavy frying pan and fry the onion until it is transparent and tender. Add the basil and cook for another minute.

Spread half of the onion mixture in the flan case and cover it with half of the courgettes, then add the remaining onion, followed by the rest of the courgettes. Sprinkle the diced cheese on top. In a bowl, whisk together the milk, eggs, salt and some black pepper. Pour this mixture over the layered vegetables. Bake until it is set and golden brown—30 to 40 minutes. Allow to cool completely before serving.

Mussel and Leek Quiche

Serves 12

Working time: about 40 minutes

Total time: about 3 hours (includes chilling)

Calories 150
Protein 10g
Cholesterol 80mg
Total fat 6g
Saturated fat 2g
Sodium 135mg

1.5 kg	mussels	**3 lb**	
175 g	baby leeks, trimmed to leave 5 cm (2 inches) of green stem, sliced into rings	**6 oz**	
30 cl	dry white wine	**½ pint**	
1 tsp	saffron threads, crushed	**1 tsp**	

2 tbsp	créme fraîche	**2 tbsp**	
15 cl	skimmed milk	**¼ pint**	
	Yogurt pastry		
140 g	plain flour	**4½ oz**	
45 g	polyunsaturated margarine	**1½ oz**	
90 g	thick Greek yogurt	**3 oz**	

Put the flour and margarine into a blender and process until fine crumbs are formed. Add the yogurt and process until the mixture becomes firm. Gather it into a ball, wrap in plastic film and chill in the refrigerator for 1 hour.

Lightly grease a 25 cm (10 inch) loose-bottomed flan tin. Spread the dough to line the tin, pressing it into an even layer over the base and sides. Place the flan case in the refrigerator.

For the filling, place the mussels, leeks and wine in a heavy saucepan. Bring the liquid to the boil, cover, and steam the mussels until the shells open. Tip the contents of the pan into a muslin-lined colander set over a bowl. Pour the reserved liquid into a clean pan and add the crushed saffron threads. Boil the liquid until it

has reduced to ¼ litre (8 fl oz), then set it aside. Remove the mussels from their shells.

Preheat the oven to 180°C (350°F or Mark 4). In a measuring jug, beat the eggs and egg yolk and whisk in the *créme fraîche*. Add the cooled saffron liquid and the skimmed milk and whisk thoroughly.

Arrange the mussels and leeks evenly in the chilled flan case, and pour on the saffron custard. Place the quiche in the oven and immediately increase the setting to 200°C (400°F or Mark 6). Bake for 15 minutes, then turn the oven setting back to 180°C (350°F or Mark 4) and cook for a further 25 to 35 minutes, until the custard is set and the pastry is golden-brown. Let it cool before slicing and serving.

Veal and Cashew Nut Rolls

Makes 8 rolls

Working time: about 45 minutes

Total time: about 2 hours (includes cooling)

Per roll:
Calories 135
Protein 16g
Cholesterol 40mg
Total fat 4g
Saturated fat 1g
Sodium 140mg

500 g	lean veal, minced	**1 lb**
250 g	carrots, grated	**8 oz**
60 g	cashew nuts, coarsely chopped	**2 oz**
	pickled gherkins, chopped	
1	lemon, grated rind and juice	**1**
1 tbsp	chopped parsley	**1 tbsp**

1 tbsp	chopped fresh sage	**1 tbsp**
¼ tsp	salt	**¼ tsp**
	freshly ground black pepper	
4	sheets phyllo pastry, each about 45 by 30 cm (18 by 12 inches)	**4**
1 tbsp	safflower oil	**1 tbsp**

Put the minced veal in a large bowl. Add the carrots, nuts, gherkins, lemon rind and juice, parsley, sage, salt and some black pepper. Combine the ingredients thoroughly. Turn the mixture on to a work surface and divide it into eight equal portions. Use your hands to roll each portion into a sausage shape.

Preheat the oven to 180°C (350°F or Mark 4). Line a baking sheet with non-stick paper.

Keeping the sheets of phyllo pastry you are not working with covered by a damp tea towel to prevent them from drying out, lay one sheet on the work surface. Brush it with a little of the safflower oil and cover it with a second sheet of phyllo. Cut this double sheet of phyllo crosswise into four equal strips, each measuring 30 by 11 cm (12 by 4½ inches). Cover the strips with a damp tea towel. Repeat with the remaining two sheets of phyllo.

Lay one of the prepared phyllo strips on the work surface and place a portion of veal and cashew nut stuffing across it at one of the short ends. Roll up the pastry and filling tightly. Using a sharp knife, make three diagonal slashes across the top of the roll. Brush the roll with safflower oil and place it on the baking sheet. Use the remaining phyllo strips and stuffing to prepare another seven rolls.

Bake the rolls until they are golden-brown— 50 minutes to 1 hour. Serve hot or cold.

Pastry Crescents with a Fish Filling

Makes about 40 crescents	
Working time: about 1 hour	
Total time: about 2 hours and 20 minutes (includes proving)	

Calories 90	
Protein 4g	
Cholesterol 20mg	
Total fat 4g	
Saturated fat 2g	
Sodium 40mg	

30 g	fresh yeast	**1 oz**		**Fish filling**	
¼ litre	skimmed milk	**8 fl oz**	**½ tsp**	unsalted butter	**½ tsp**
75 g	unsalted butter	**2½ oz**	**1**	shallot or small onion, chopped	**1**
500 g	strong plain flour	**1 lb**	**30 cl**	unsalted fish stock	**½ pint**
½ tsp	salt	**½ tsp**	**250 g**	herring fillet	**8 oz**
1	egg, plus a little beaten egg	**1**	**250 g**	salmon or salmon trout fillet	**8 oz**
2 tbsp	caraway seeds, for garnish	**2 tbsp**	**2 tbsp**	finely chopped fresh dill	**2 tbsp**

Cream the fresh yeast with 1 tablespoon of warm water and set aside for 10 minutes until activated. Warm the milk and butter in a saucepan. Sift the flour with the salt, make a well and beat in the milk and butter, yeast mixture and egg. Knead until the dough feels elastic—about 10 minutes. Cover with plastic film and set aside in a warm place until it is double its original volume—1 to 1½ hours.

Heat the butter in a frying pan over low heat; add the shallot and sauté gently for 10 minutes. Bring the stock to the boil, add the herring and salmon, and poach over low heat until the fish is just cooked through—about 3 minutes. Remove the fish from the pan with a slotted

spoon, skin it and flake the flesh. Mix the fish and the dill into the shallots, and set aside.

Knock back the yeast dough and knead it briefly. Roll out half the dough on a floured surface to form a rectangle approximately 40 by 28 cm (16 by 11 inches). Using a round pastry cutter, cut out about 20 circles. Place some filling in the centre of each; wet the edges and bring the two halves together. Press to seal the edges, and bend the semi-circles to form crescents. Repeat with the remaining dough.

Brush the crescents with the beaten egg and sprinkle with the caraway seeds. Preheat the oven to 200°C (400°F or Mark 6). Bake until golden-brown—10 to 12 minutes. Serve warm.

Miniature Samosas

Makes 32
samosas

Working
(and total)
time: about 1
hour and 15
minutes

Per samosa:
Calories
25
Protein
1g
Cholesterol
3mg
Total fat
1g
Saturated fat
1g
Sodium
35mg

250 g	potatoes, peeled and chopped	8 oz	$\frac{1}{2}$ tsp	salt	$\frac{1}{2}$ tsp
90 g	carrots, sliced	3 oz	$\frac{1}{8}$ tsp	cayenne pepper	$\frac{1}{8}$ tsp
7 g	dried ceps, soaked for 20 minutes in hot water	$\frac{1}{4}$ oz	4	sheets phyllo pastry, each about 45 by 30 cm (18 by 12 inches)	4
1 tsp	poppy seeds	1 tsp		coriander sprigs, for garnish	
40 g	unsalted butter	$1\frac{1}{4}$ oz		**Coriander-yogurt dip**	
1	small onion, finely chopped	1	15	coriander sprigs, leaves only, finely chopped	15
60 g	shelled young fresh peas	2 oz			
1 cm	ginger root, finely chopped	$\frac{1}{2}$ inch	$\frac{1}{4}$ litre	plain low-fat yogurt	8 fl oz
$\frac{1}{2}$ tsp	garam masala	$\frac{1}{2}$ tsp		freshly ground black pepper	

Boil the potatoes and carrots separately until they are tender. Drain and leave to cool. Dice the carrots and mash the potatoes. Drain and squeeze dry the ceps, and chop them finely.

Toast the poppy seeds in a dry frying pan until they change colour. Remove from heat.

Melt 7 g ($\frac{1}{4}$ oz) of butter in a heavy frying pan and brown the onion. Add the peas, mushrooms and ginger, and cook for 2 to 3 minutes. Add the potatoes and carrots, and mix well. Remove from the heat, stir in the garam masala, salt and cayenne pepper, and set aside.

Preheat the oven to 200°C (400°F or Mark 6). Cut one sheet of phyllo into eight strips. Keep the phyllo you are not working on covered with a damp cloth. Melt the remaining butter and lightly brush one side of each strip, then make up the strips into triangular packages, each with about 1 teaspoon of filling. Bake in for 15 to 20 minutes, until golden-brown.

To make the dip, mix the coriander into the yogurt and season with some pepper. Serve the samosas hot, garnished with the coriander sprigs and accompanied by the dip.

Vegetable Wholemeal Pizza

Serves 4

Working time: about 25 minutes

Total time: about 45 minutes

Calories 250
Protein 12g
Cholesterol 10mg
Total fat 9g
Saturated fat 3g
Sodium 420mg

¼ tsp	dried yeast	¼ tsp	
175 g	wholemeal flour	6 oz	
¼ tsp	salt	¼ tsp	
15 g	polyunsaturated margarine	½ oz	
3	tomatoes, quartered	3	
1	small onion, chopped	1	
1 tsp	virgin olive oil	1 tsp	

	freshly ground black pepper	
1	courgette, sliced	1
5	sweet red pepper rings	5
4	baby sweetcorn	4
60 g	mushrooms, sliced	2 oz
1 tsp	dried oregano	1 tsp
60 g	low-fat mozzarella, grated	2 oz

Reconstitute the dried yeast according to the manufacturer's instructions. Sift the flour and ⅛teaspoon of the salt into a bowl, adding back the bran from the sieve. Rub in the margarine, then make a well in the centre; pour in the yeast and mix it in to make a dough that can be formed into a ball. Knead until smooth and elastic—5 to 10 minutes. Put it in a bowl, cover with plastic film and microwave for 10 seconds. Leave for 10 minutes, then microwave again for 10 seconds and leave to rise for 10 minutes.

Place the tomatoes on a plate. Microwave on high for 1 to 2 minutes, then peel and chop. Put the onion in a bowl with ½ teaspoon of the oil and microwave on high for 2 minutes. Add the tomatoes and season with the remaining salt and pepper. Set aside.

Put the other vegetables in a bowl with 1 tablespoon of water; cover with plastic film, leaving one corner open, and cook on high for 3 minutes. Drain the vegetables.

Knead the dough for 1 minute, then roll it out into a 25 cm (10 inch) circle. Brush a plate with the remaining oil and place the dough on the plate. Spread on the tomato and onion mixture and arrange the other vegetables over the top. Sprinkle on the oregano and mozzarella. Microwave the pizza on high for 10 seconds, then rest it for 5 minutes. Cook on high for 5 to 6 minutes. Rest for 5 minutes before serving.

Chicken and Walnut Pizzas

Serves 6

Working time: about 45 minutes

Total time: about 2 hours

Calories 365
Protein 19g
Cholesterol 30mg
Total fat 15g
Saturated fat 3g
Sodium 180mg

3	chicken thighs (about 350g/12 oz)	3
1	carrot, coarsely chopped	1
1	large onion, coarsely chopped, plus 1 tsp finely chopped onion	1
6	black peppercorns	6
1	thyme sprig	1
1	bay leaf	1
75 g	shelled walnuts	2 oz
1	garlic clove, finely chopped	
⅛ tsp	cayenne pepper	⅛ tsp

⅛ tsp	paprika	⅛ tsp
¼ tsp	salt	¼ tsp
½	sweet red pepper, cored, denbbed, seeded and sliced into rings	½
	parsley for garnish	
	Pizza dough	
15 g	fresh yeast	½ oz
300 g	plain flour	10 oz
¼ tsp	salt	¼ tsp
1 tbsp	virgin olive oil	1 tbsp

Mix the yeast with water and leave for 10 to 15 minutes. Sift the flour and salt into a bowl. Pour in the yeast together with the oil. Mix in water to make a pliable dough. Knead until smooth and elastic. Form it into a ball, cover, and leave to rise—about 1 hour.

Put the chicken in a saucepan and cover with water. Add the carrot, chopped onion, peppercorns, thyme and bay leaf. Bring to the boil, cover and simmer for 15 to 20 minutes.

Preheat the oven to 220°C (425°F or Mark 7) and lightly oil two baking sheets. Deflate the dough, then roll out six ovals. Shape raised rims, then put on the baking sheets and leave.

Strain the chicken stock into a bowl. Skin and bone the chicken and chop the meat.

Finely chop the walnuts, then mix in the finely chopped onion, the garlic, cayenne pepper, paprika and salt. Add 15 cl (¼ pint) stock to make a smooth sauce when blended.

Divide the sauce among the bases and bake for 10 to 15 minutes. Sprinkle with the chicken and pepper rings, then return to the oven for 5 to 10 minutes. Garnish with parsley.

32

Tuna Tapenade Pizzas

Serves 6

Working time:
about 40
minutes

Total time:
about 2 hours
(includes
proving)

Calories
340
Protein
14g
Cholesterol
25mg
Total fat
15g
Saturated fat
2g
Sodium
305mg

15 g	fresh yeast	½ oz
300 g	plain flour	10 oz
1 tsp	salt	1 tsp
1 tbsp	virgin olive oil	1 tbsp
6	cherry tomatoes. sliced, for garnish	6
	chopped parsley, for garnish	
	Tuna tapenade	
3	anchovy fillets, rinsed, dried and finely chopped	3

1	garlic clove, finely chopped	1
1½ tbsp	capers, chopped	1½ tbsp
12	black olives, stoned, finely chopped	12
200 g	tuna fish canned, drained	7oz
1 tbsp	virgin olive oil	1 tbsp
	freshly ground black pepper	

Mix the yeast with 15 cl (¼ pint) of tepid water and leave for 10 to 15 minutes. Sift the flour and salt into a large bowl and make a well in the flour. When the yeast solution is frothy, pour it into the well along with the oil and mix in enough tepid water to make a soft, firm dough. Knead the dough until it is smooth and elastic— about 10 minutes—then gather it into a ball and leave in a clean bowl, covered with plastic film, until doubled in size—about 1 hour.

Preheat the oven to 220°C (425°F or Mark 7) and lightly oil a baking tray. Knock the dough back, then divide it into six balls. On a floured work surface, roll out each ball into a circle. Press the edges of the circles to create a raised rim. Put the circles on the prepared baking tray and leave to rise a little—at least 10 minutes.

For the tapenade, pound the anchovies and garlic together in a mortar. Add the capers, olives, tuna fish, oil and some pepper in gradual stages, continuing to pound to form a paste. Divide the paste equally among the pizza bases and spread it to within 5 mm (¼ inch) of the edges. Bake for 15 minutes, then garnish with the tomato slices and return to the oven for 5 minutes. Serve warm, garnished with parsley.

Pissaladière Tartlets

Makes 24
tartlets

Working time
about 1 hour

Total time:
about 1 hour
and 45
minutes

Per tartlet:
Calories
70
Protein
2g
Cholesterol
trace
Total fat
3g
Saturated fat
trace
Sodium
45mg

1½ tbsp	virgin olive oil	1½ tbsp
2	onions, quartered, sliced	2
1	garlic clove, finely chopped	1
6	anchovy fillets, soaked in milk for 30 minutes, rinsed in cold water	6
12	black olives, stoned, quartered	12

Tartlet dough		
15 g	fresh yeast	½ oz
250 g	strong plain flour	8 oz
¼ tsp	salt	¼ tsp
1½ tbsp	virgin olive oil	1½ tbsp
1 tsp	chopped fresh rosemary	1 tsp

First prepare the dough. Dissolve the fresh yeast in 2 tablespoons of tepid water. Sift the flour and salt into a bowl, make a well in the centre and pour in the yeast solution. Add 1 tablespoon of the oil, the rosemary and 12.5 cl (4 fl oz) of tepid water, and mix to make a soft dough. Knead the dough until it is smooth and elastic—about 5 minutes.

Put the remaining ½ tablespoon of oil in a mixing bowl. Form the dough into a ball and put it into the bowl and coat with oil. Cover with a damp tea towel and leave in a warm place to rise—about 1 hour.

While the dough rises, prepare the filling. Heat the oil in a large frying pan and sauté the onion and garlic for 40 minutes over low heat, adding a little water if necessary to prevent them from sticking.

Cut each anchovy fillet lengthwise into four strips then halve again by cutting across them.

Preheat the oven to 200°C (400°F or Mark 6). Knock back the dough, then turn it out on to a floured surface and knead briefly. Cut the into 2 portions and roll out each into a circle about 6 cm (2½ inches) in diameter. Use the circles to line 6 cm (2½ inches) diameter tartlet tins.

Fill each dough case with a heaped teaspoon of the onion mixture and smooth the surface. Cross two anchovy strips on each tartlet, and add two olive quarters. Place on a baking sheet and bake until the dough has risen and is lightly golden—about 15 minutes. Serve hot.

Spinach Cocktail Quiches

Makes 18 quiches

Working time: about 1 hour

Total time: about 1 hour and 20 minutes

Per quiche:
Calories 140
Protein 5g
Cholesterol 35mg
Total fat 9g
Saturated fat 3g
Sodium 165mg

175 g	flour	**6 oz**
¾ tsp	salt	**¾ tsp**
90 g	polyunsaturated margarine	**3 oz**
1	egg white, lightly beaten	**1**
¼ litre	skimmed milk	**8 fl oz**
	freshly ground black pepper	
60 g	Parmesan cheese, grated	**2 oz**

	Spinach filling	
3 tbsp	virgin olive oil	**3 tbsp**
2	onions, finely chopped	**2**
2	sweet red peppers, chopped	**2**
2	sweet green peppers, chopped	**2**
750 g	spinach leaves, washed	**6 oz**

To make the dough, sift the flour and ⅛ teaspoon of the salt into a bowl, then rub in the margarine until the mixture resembles fine breadcrumbs. Add the egg white and mix. Knead the dough until smooth.

Roll out the dough then, using a 10 cm (4 inch) plain round cutter, cut out rounds. Fit the rounds into fluted tartlet tins. Place the tins on baking sheets and refrigerate.

Heat the oil in a small, heavy frying pan, add the onion and sweet peppers, and cook for 6 to 8 minutes, until soft. Meanwhile, bring a small saucepan of water to the boil, plunge the spinach leaves into the water and bring back to the boil for 30 seconds. Drain the spinach

in a colander, then rinse under cold running water to refresh it. Squeeze the spinach dry and chop finely. Put the spinach and the pepper mixture into a small bowl and set aside.

Preheat the oven to 220°C (425°F or Mark 7). Put the eggs and milk into a bowl, and season with the remaining salt and a little pepper. Whisk lightly together, then stir in the Parmesan cheese. Divide the egg mixture equally among the three bowls of filling and mix each one thoroughly.

Fill the pastry-lined tins with the spinach mixture. Bake in the oven until they are golden-brown and the filling set—20 to 25 minutes. Serve warm.

Buckwheat Blinis Topped with Goat Cheese

Makes about 60 blinis

Working time: about 45 minutes

Total time: about 2 hours and 30 minutes

Per blini:
Calories 35
Protein 2g
Cholesterol 10mg
Total fat 2g
Saturated fat trace
Sodium 65mg

35 cl	skimmed milk	12 fl oz
15 g	fresh yeast	½ oz
125 g	buckwheat flour	4 oz
125 g	strong plain flour	4 oz
¼ tsp	salt	¼ tsp
½ tsp	ground caraway seeds	½ tsp
½ tsp	crushed black sesame seeds	½ tsp
2 tsp	honey	2 tsp

½ tbsp	unsalted butter	½ tbsp
1	egg, separated	1
	Goat cheese topping	
250 g	soft goat cheese	8 oz
1½ tsp	sesame seeds, toasted	1½ tsp
1 tbsp	caraway seeds, toasted	1 tbsp
1 tbsp	poppy seeds, toasted	1 tbsp
2 tbsp	sunflower seeds, toasted	2 tbsp

Warm 2 tablespoons of the milk, blend in the fresh yeast, and leave for about 10 to 15 minutes for the yeast to activate.

Sift the flours and salt into a bowl, stir in the caraway and sesame seeds, and make a hollow in the mixture. In a small pan, warm the remaining milk with the honey and butter.

Remove from the heat and stir in the yeast mixture. Pour the milk and yeast mixture, together with the egg yolk, into the flour and blend, gradually incorporating the flour. Beat for a further 2 minutes. Leave in a warm place for about 1 hour until well risen and bubbly. The batter should drop easily from a teaspoon;

if it is too stiff, beat in a little warm water. Whisk the egg white and fold it into the batter.

Heat a large griddle or frying pan over medium heat. Drop the batter a teaspoon at a time on to the griddle or frying pan, and spread the batter into rounds about 5 cm (2 inches) in diameter. Cook the blinis until they are covered with bubbles and the undersides are quite dry and golden. Flip over and repeat. Wrap up each batch of blinis in a folded cloth napkin, and keep warm.

For the topping, beat the cheese to a smooth, even texture. Drop a half teaspoon on each blini, and sprinkle each with one type of seed.

Curried Vegetable Pancakes with Yogurt

Makes
about 30
Pancakes

Working
(and total)
time: about
1 hour

Per pancake:
Calories
25
Protein
10g
Cholesterol
1mg
Total fat
1g
Saturated fat
trace
Sodium
40mg

60 g	plain flour	**2 oz**	**1 tbsp**	grapeseed or safflower oil	**1 tbsp**
60 g	wholemeal flour	**2 oz**	**100 g**	sweet potato, peeled and grated	**3½ oz**
½ tsp	baking powder	**½ tsp**	**100 g**	celeriac, peeled and grated	**3½ oz**
½ tsp	salt	**½ tsp**	**Coriander-lime yogurt topping**		
1 tsp	punch puran	**1 tsp**	**175 g**	thick Greek yogurt	**6 oz**
1 tsp	garam masala	**1 tsp**	**⅛ tsp**	salt	**⅛ tsp**
1 tsp	ground turmeric	**1 tsp**	**1 tsp**	lime pickle	**1 tsp**
½ tsp	ground cardamom	**½ tsp**	**½ tsp**	freshly grated lime rind	**½ tsp**
12.5 cl	plain low-fat yogurt	**4 fl oz**	**1**	small bunch fresh coriander, chopped	**1**

Mix together all the ingredients for the coriander-lime yogurt topping. Pour into a serving bowl and chill in the refrigerator.

To make the batter, first sift the flours, baking powder and salt into a bowl. Dry-fry the punch puran in a heavy frying pan until it smells highly aromatic—about 2 minutes. Add it to the flour with the garam masala, turmeric and cardamom, stir, and make a hollow in the centre of the flour. Mix the yogurt with 12.5 cl (4 fl oz) of water and pour into the well together with the oil. Blend, gradually incorporating the dry ingredients into the liquid. Beat lightly until no lumps remain. Stir in the sweet potato and celeriac.

Set a griddle or frying pan over medium heat. Drop tablespoons of the batter on to the griddle and use the back of the spoon to spread it into rounds. Cook the pancakes gently, a few at a time, over medium heat for 4 to 5 minutes on each side, until lightly browned. Transfer to a platter, cover loosely with foil and keep warm in a 170°C (325°F or Mark 3) oven while you cook the remaining batter.

Serve the warm pancakes topped with a teaspoon of the coriander-lime yogurt.

Raised Pies with Carrot and Broccoli Filling

Serves 6	
Working time: about 1 hour	
Total time: about 2 hours	

Calories 450
Protein 17g
Cholesterol 110mg
Total fat 25g
Saturated fat 6g
Sodium 375mg

500 g	carrots, chopped	**1 lb**
1	egg, beaten	**1**
60 g	pine-nuts, ground	**2 oz**
150 g	low-fat fromage frais	**5 oz**
¼ tsp	salt	**¼ tsp**
	freshly ground black pepper	
125 g	broccoli florets	**4 oz**

½	bunch watercress, chopped	**½**
2 tbsp	skimmed milk, for glazing	**2 tbsp**
	Hot-water crust pastry	
350 g	wholemeal flour	**12 oz**
60 g	polyunsaturated margarine	**2 oz**
60 g	hard white vegetable fat, diced	**2 oz**

Steam the carrots over a saucepan of boiling water until they are tender. Mash and transfer to a bowl. Mix in the beaten egg, pine-nuts, *fromage frais*, salt and some black pepper. Steam the broccoli until tender, then chop and transfer to a bowl. Stir in the watercress.

Preheat the oven to 200°C (400°F or Mark 6). Lightly grease six 15 cl (¼ pint) ramekins.

To make the pastry, place the flour in a large bowl and make a well in the centre. Put the egg yolk into the well. Gently heat the margarine, vegetable fat and 17.5 cl (6 fl oz) of water in a small saucepan, until the fat melts. Bring the liquid to a rolling boil and pour into the well, stirring to mix the ingredients to a soft

dough. Knead on a lightly floured surface until smooth, then cut off one third. Wrap this in plastic film and set it aside.

Divide the large piece of dough into six. Roll out each one on a lightly floured surface into a circle large enough to line a ramekin.

Distribute half of the carrot mixture among the pastry cases, cover with the broccoli mixture then another carrot layer. Make lids with the reserved dough. Press the edges firmly together and flute the edges. Cut a hole in the top of each and glaze with the skimmed milk.

Bake the pies for 40 minutes, until the pastry is crisp. Remove from the oven and allow to stand for 3 to 4 minutes before serving.

Savoury Pumpkin Pie

Serves 6

Working time: about 30 minutes

Total time: about 1 hour and 15 minutes

Calories 175
Protein 13g
Cholesterol 75mg
Total fat 3g
Saturated fat 1g
Sodium 80mg

500 g	pumpkin, peeled and diced	**1 lb**
200 g	quark	**7 oz**
2	eggs, beaten	**2**
1	onion, sliced into rings	**1**
1½ tsp	safflower oil	**1½ tsp**
1	garlic clove, crushed	**1**
½ tsp	ground ginger	**½ tsp**

½ tsp	chili powder	**½ tsp**
⅛ tsp	salt	**⅛ tsp**
	white pepper	
	Yeast dough	
175 g	wholemeal flour	**6 oz**
1 tsp	easy-blend dried yeast	**1 tsp**
12.5 cl	skimmed milk	**4 fl oz**

To make the dough, mix together the flour and yeast in a bowl. Heat the milk in a saucepan until it is hot to the touch—about 43°C (110°F)—then pour it into the dry ingredients. Knead the mixture well for 10 minutes, adding a little extra water if necessary, to make a smooth, soft dough. Leave the dough to rest for 10 minutes. Roll out the dough and use it to line a lightly greased 20 cm (8 inch) flan tin.

Preheat the oven to 200°C (400°F or Mark 6).

Steam the pumpkin over a saucepan of boiling water until they are soft. Transfer to a bowl and mash. When the purée has cooled, beat in the quark and eggs.

Meanwhile, set a quarter of the onion rings

aside and chop the remainder. Heat the oil in a small, heavy-bottomed saucepan over medium heat. Add the chopped onion and garlic, and sauté them for about 3 minutes, until softened but not browned. Stir in the ginger and chili powder.

Transfer the pumpkin mixture to a food processor, and add the contents of the saucepan, the salt and some pepper. Blend the mixture until it is smooth. Pour the filling into the pastry case and level the surface. Press the reserved onion rings lightly into the filling and brush them with the extra safflower oil.

Bake the pie for 30 to 40 minutes, until it is golden-brown and firm in the centre.

Mustard Cauliflower Flan

Serves 4

Working time: about 40 minutes

Total time: about 1 hour and 30 minutes

Calories 330

Protein 11g

Cholesterol 55mg

Total fat 15g

Saturated fat 4g

Sodium 285mg

1	cauliflower trimmed and divided into small florets	1
1 tsp	virgin olive oil	1 tsp
1	onion, finely chopped	1
1	large cooking apple, peeled, cored and chopped	1
1½ tbsp	Dijon mustard	1½ tbsp
2 tbsp	plain flour	2 tbsp
1	egg, lightly beaten	1

30 cl	skimmed milk	½ pint
¼ tsp	salt	¼ tsp
	white pepper	
	paprika	
	Herb pastry	
125 g	wholemeal flour	4 oz
60 g	margarine, chilled	2 oz
2 tbsp	finely chopped fresh coriander	2 tbsp
2 tbsp	finely chopped flat-leaf parsley	2 tbsp

Put the flour in a mixing bowl and rub in the margarine until the mixture resembles fine breadcrumbs. Stir in the coriander and parsley. Blend in 3 to 4 tablespoons of water to form a dough. Gather into a ball and knead until it is smooth. Roll out the dough and line a flan tin 20 cm (8 inches) in diameter, and about 4 cm (1½ inches) deep. Prick the pastry with a fork, and chill it in the refrigerator for 30 minutes. Preheat the oven to 200°C (400°F or Mark 6).

Bake the pastry case for 10 to 15 minutes, until crisp. Remove from the oven and reduce the temperature to 180°C (350°F or Mark 4).

Meanwhile, parboil the cauliflower until just tender—about 5 minutes. Drain, rinse, and drain again. Set the florets aside. Fry the onion until transparent. Add the apple and cook for another 4 minutes, until just tender.

Spread the onion and apple mixture inside the flan case and arrange the cauliflower on top. Blend the mustard and flour to form a smooth paste. Using an electric whisk, beat in the egg and milk. Add the salt and some pepper, and pour the mixture into the flan case.

Bake in the oven for 30 to 45 minutes. Serve the flan sprinkled with a little paprika.

Granary Pizza with Sweetcorn and Pineapple

Serves 4		
Working time: about 40 minutes		
Total time: about 1 hour and 45 minutes		

Calories 395	
Protein 17g	
Cholesterol 15mg	
Total fat 8g	
Saturated fat 4g	
Sodium 390mg	

2 tbsp	grainy mustard	2 tbsp	
350 g	sweetcorn kernels	12 oz	
½ tsp	safflower oil	½ tsp	
1	large onion, sliced into rings	1	
2 tsp	chopped fresh basil, plus shredded basil, for garnish	2 tsp	
⅛ tsp	paprika	⅛ tsp	
½	small ripe pineapple, skinned, cored and diced	½	

1	sweet orange or red pepper, seeded, deribbed and diced		1
4	black olives, stoned and quartered		4
90 g	Gouda cheese grated		3 oz
	Pizza Dough		
125 g	granary flour		4 oz
125 g	plain flour		4 oz
½ tsp	salt		½ tsp
30 g	fresh yeast, or 1 tsp dried yeast		1 oz

Mix both types of flour in a bowl with the salt. In a small bowl, crumble the fresh yeast over 15 cl (¼ pint) of warm water. Leave the mixture in a warm place for about 10 minutes. Make a well in the centre of the dry ingredients and pour in the yeast. Mix to a soft dough and knead for 5 minutes. Cover with plastic film and leave in a warm place for about 10 minutes.

Knock back the dough, then roll it out on a floured surface into a circle. Place on a lightly greased baking sheet. Brush with the mustard, leaving a border of dough. Cover and leave in a warm place for about 10 minutes.

Preheat the oven to 200°C (400°F or Mark 6). Cook the sweetcorn in a pan of simmering water for 3 minutes, then drain. Heat the oil in a heavy frying pan over medium heat. Add the onion rings and fry them gently for 5 to 6 minutes, until soft. Stir in the chopped basil.

Arrange the onion and basil over the pizza base and sprinkle on the paprika. Scatter on the sweetcorn and pineapple. Add the sweet pepper and olives, and sprinkle with cheese.

Bake the pizza for 20 to 25 minutes, until the dough is crusty round the edges. Serve hot, garnished with the shredded basil leaves.

Broccoli and Pecorino Pasties

Serves 8

Working time:
about 1 hour

Total time:
about 2 hours
and 15
minutes

Calories
320
Protein
12g
Cholesterol
60mg
Total fat
13g
Saturated fat
5g
Sodium
150mg

1 tsp	virgin olive oil	1 tsp	45 g	pecorino cheese, finely grated	1½ oz
1	red onion, finely chopped	1	¼ tsp	salt	¼ tsp
300 g	purple-sprouting broccoli stalks and leaves chopped	10 oz		**Lemon shortcrust pastry**	
			400 g	plain flour	14 oz
100 g	kale, stemmed and chopped	3½ oz	2 tbsp	virgin olive oil	2 tbsp
200 g	tomatoes, skinned and chopped	7 oz	30 g	unsalted butter	1 oz
¼	hot chili pepper, chopped	¼	2	eggs, beaten	2
1 tbsp	pine-nuts, toasted	1 tbsp	½	lemon, juice only, made up to 14 cl (4½ fl oz) with warm water	½
100 g	low-fat ricotta cheese	3½ oz			

Sift the flour into a bowl and rub in the olive oil and butter until the mixture resembles fine breadcrumbs. Make a well in the centre and pour in three quarters of the beaten eggs, and the diluted lemon juice. Mix well, then gather the dough into a ball and knead until smooth. Cover with a tea towel and leave to rest in a cool place for at least an hour.

Gently heat the oil in a heavy saucepan and cook the onion until transparent. Steam the broccoli and kale over a saucepan of boiling water, until they are no longer tough—about 5 minutes. Drain well, then toss them with the onion and leave to cool a little. Stir in the tomatoes, chili, pine-nuts, cheeses and salt.

Divide the dough into two. Roll out each piece into a rectangle measuring approximately 90 by 22 cm (36 by 9 inches). Using a round plate as a guide, cut out four circles.

Preheat the oven to 200°C (400°F or Mark 6). Place one eighth of the filling slightly off-centre on each round of dough, then fold . Pinch the edges and brush with the remaining beaten egg and place them on a baking sheet. Bake for about 25 minutes, until they are a light golden colour. Serve them hot.

Asparagus Strudel

Serves 4

Working time:
about 40
minutes

Total time:
about 1 hour
and 10
minutes

Calories
225
Protein
10g
Cholesterol
60mg
Total fat
13g
Saturated fat
5g
Sodium
380mg

350 g	asparagus, trimmed, peeled, sliced diagonally	**12 oz**	**¼ tsp**	salt	**¼ tsp**
				freshly ground black pepper	
175 g	low-fat soft cheese	**6 oz**	**5**	sheets phyllo pastry, about 45 by 30 cm (18 by 12 inches)	**5**
2 tbsp	finely cut chives	**2 tbsp**			
2 tbsp	chopped fresh marjoram	**2 tbsp**	**30 g**	margarine, melted	**1 oz**
1 tbsp	chopped parsley	**1 tbsp**	**30 g**	fresh wholemeal breadcrumbs	**1 oz**
1	egg, separated	**1**			

Place the asparagus pieces in a steamer set over a saucepan of boiling water and steam them for 5 to 6 minutes, until they are tender. Refresh them under cold running water and drain.

Put the soft cheese into a bowl with the herbs, egg yolk, salt and some black pepper. Beat the ingredients together well and stir in the drained asparagus. In a clean bowl, whisk the egg white until it is stiff, then fold it carefully into the asparagus mixture.

Preheat the oven to 200°C (400°F or Mark 6). Lightly grease a baking sheet.

Lay one phyllo sheet out flat on the work surface, with a long side towards you. Cover the other sheets with a damp cloth. Brush a little of the margarine over the sheet on the work surface and sprinkle with one fifth of the breadcrumbs. Lay the other phyllo sheets on top of the first, repeating this process.

Spoon the asparagus mixture on to the top sheet of phyllo, mounding it in a line about 2.5 cm (1 inch) in from the edge nearest to you, leaving about 2.5 cm (1 inch) clear at each end.

Fold the sides of the pastry in, over the asparagus mixture, then loosely roll up to enclose the filling. Place the strudel, with the join underneath, on the prepared baking sheet. Brush the remaining margarine over the top .

Bake the strudel for 25 to 30 minutes, until it is golden-brown. Serve it either warm or cold.

Burghul-Stuffed Phyllo Packages

Serves 4

Working time: about 35 minutes

Total time: about 1 hour and 45 minutes (includes soaking)

Calories 315
Protein 10g
Cholesterol 0mg
Total fat 10g
Saturated fat 2g
Sodium 115mg

125 g	burghul, soaked in 60 cl (1 pint) hot water for 1 hour	**4 oz**
175 g	carrots, grated	**6 oz**
6	dried apricots, chopped	**6**
1 tbsp	currants	**1 tbsp**
60 g	unsalted cashew nuts, chopped	**2 oz**
½ tsp	ground cumin	**½ tsp**

½ tsp	ground coriander	**½ tsp**
2 tbsp	finely chopped parsley	**2 tbsp**
⅛ tsp	salt	**⅛ tsp**
	freshly ground black pepper	
5	sheets phyllo pastry, each about 45 by 30 cm (18 by 12 inches)	**5**
2 tsp	safflower oil	**2 tsp**

Preheat the oven to 200°C (400°F or Mark 6). Lightly grease a baking sheet.

Drain the burghul well, pressing out as much moisture as possible. Place in a large bowl and add the carrots, apricots, currants, cashew nuts, cumin, coriander, parsley, salt and some black pepper. Mix well.

Lay out one sheet of phyllo pastry on the work surface; keep the other sheets covered by a clean, damp cloth while you work, to prevent them from drying out. Brush a little oil over the sheet on the work surface. Place a quarter of the burghul mixture near one end of the sheet, half way between the two longer sides, and flatten it down gently. Fold the shorter edge of the pastry over the filling, fold in the two longer side edges, then roll the stuffed section up to the other end, to form a package. Place the package on the baking sheet, with the join underneath. Roll up another three phyllo packages in the same way.

Cut the remaining sheet of phyllo pastry into strips. Crumple the strips loosely in your hand, and use some to decorate the top of each package. Brush the remaining oil or a little skimmed milk over the packages, and bake them in the oven for 20 to 25 minutes, until they are golden-brown.

Lamb and Courgette Pie

Serves 6

Working time:
about 1 hour

Total time.
about 2 hours
and 25
minutes

Calories
240
Protein
21g
Cholesterol
75mg
Total fat
12g
Saturated fat
4g
Sodium
220mg

500 g	lean lamb, trimmed and diced	**1 lb**	**¼ litre**	unsalted brown stock	**8 fl oz**
1 tbsp	virgin olive oil	**1 tbsp**	**1 tsp**	mixed dried herbs	**1 tsp**
1	large onion, finely chopped	**1**	**½ tsp**	salt	**½ tsp**
2	garlic cloves, crushed	**2**		freshly ground black pepper	
250 g	carrots, diced	**8 oz**	**5**	sheets phyllo pastry, each	**5**
250 g	courgettes, diced	**8 oz**		45 by 30 cm (18 by 12 inches)	
30 g	plain flour	**1 oz**	**30 g**	margarine, melted	**1 oz**

Heat the oil in a large, heavy sauté pan over medium heat. Add the onion, garlic and carrots. Reduce the heat to low and cook gently until the vegetables are soft but not brown. Increase the heat to high, then add the diced lamb. Stir to keep the pieces of meat separated, until the lamb changes colour—1 to 2 minutes. Add the courgettes, then stir in the flour, stock, mixed herbs, salt and pepper to taste. Bring the liquid to the boil, stirring. Reduce the heat to low, cover, and simmer until the courgettes are soft—8 to 10 minutes. Remove the pan from the heat and allow to cool for about 45 minutes.

Preheat the oven to 220°C (425°F or Mark 7). Pour the mixture into a 20 cm (8 inch) pie plate.

Cut four of the phyllo sheets in half widthwise. Brush the edge of the pie plate with a little cold water, then cover the meat mixture with one of the half phyllo sheets, brush the phyllo with a little of the melted margarine and cover it with another sheet of phyllo. Repeat with the remaining six half sheets of phyllo. Cut the pastry to fit the dish exactly.

Use the remaining phyllo to make decorative diamond shapes. Brush them with the margarine so that they stay in place. Make a small hole in the centre of the pie.

Place the pie on a baking sheet and cook it in the oven until the pastry is golden-brown—35 to 40 minutes. Serve immediately

Fillet of Beef Wrapped in Phyllo

Serves 8

Working time:
about 40
minutes

Total time:
about 3 hours
and 15
minutes

Calories
300
Protein
32g
Cholesterol
65mg
Total fat
12g
Saturated fat
4g
Sodium
75 mg

1 kg	beef fillet, trimmed and tied	**2¼ lb**
3 tbsp	virgin olive oil	**3 tbsp**
1 tsp	mixed dried herbs	**1 tsp**
1	garlic clove, crushed	**1**
	freshly ground black pepper	
4 tbsp	red wine	**4 tbsp**
1	onion, finely chopped	**1**
250 g	button mushrooms, chopped	**8 oz**
2 tbsp	chopped parsley	**2 tbsp**
200 g	phyllo pastry (about 7 sheets, 30 by 45 cm/12 by 18 inches)	**7 oz**
15 g	butter, melted	**½ oz**
	cooked mushrooms to garnish	

In a shallow dish, blend 1 tablespoon of the oil with the herbs, garlic and pepper. Add the beef and coat evenly. Cover and marinate at room temperature for at least 1 hour.

Heat another tablespoon of the oil in a non-stick sauté pan or frying pan over high heat. Brown the beef on all sides—about 5 to 8 minutes—then transfer it to a plate. Strain off all the fat from the pan and stir in 2 tablespoons of the wine. Bring to the boil and boil until reduced by half—about 1 minute. Pour over the beef and set the meat aside until cold.

Meanwhile, heat the remaining oil in the pan over medium heat, add the onion and cook gently for 5 to 6 minutes until softened, but not browned. Add the mushrooms and cook until they are softened—6 to 8 minutes. Stir the remaining wine into the mushrooms, bring to the boil and cook until all the juices in the pan have evaporated—about 5 minutes. Stir in the parsley. Set aside to cool.

Heat the oven to 230°C (450°F or Mark 8). Lay the phyllo pastry sheets out flat, one on top of another, and cut a 5 cm (2 inch) wide strip from one side. Cut it into diamond shapes. Fill the phyllo with the mushroom mixture and beef fillet and make a neat parcel.

Bake for 35 minutes until golden-brown. Carefully remove to a serving dish and garnish with mushrooms. Serve immediately.

Suetcrust Steak and Chestnut Pie

Serves 6

Working time:
about 45 minutes

Total time:
about 2 hours
and 45 minutes
(includes cooling)

Calories
300
Protein
21g
Cholesterol
45mg
Total fat
20g
Saturated fat
5g
Sodium
140mg

500 g	rump steak, trimmed and cubed	**1 lb**	**6**	carrots, sliced	**6**
1	onion, sliced	**1**	**4**	sticks celery, sliced diagonally	**4**
8 cl	fresh orange juice	**3 fl oz**	**250 g**	button mushrooms, wiped	**8 oz**
12.5 cl	brown stock	**4 fl oz**	**½ tbsp**	skimmed milk, to glaze	**½ tbsp**
½	orange, grated rind only	**½**		**Suetcrust**	
125 g	dried chestnuts, soaked overnight	**4 oz**	**175 g**	plain flour	**6 oz**
1 tbsp	tomato paste	**1 tbsp**	**1½ tsp**	baking powder	**1½ tsp**
1 tsp	chopped fresh thyme	**1 tsp**	**½ tsp**	dry mustard	**½ tsp**
	freshly ground black pepper		**⅛ tsp**	salt	**⅛ tsp**
⅛ tsp	salt	**⅛ tsp**	**90 g**	vegetarian suet	**3 oz**

Put the steak and sliced onion in a casserole with the orange juice and stock. Bring to the boil, then add the orange rind, chestnuts, tomato paste, thyme, pepper and salt. Reduce the heat, cover and simmer for 30 minutes. Add the carrots and celery and simmer for 30 minutes. Remove from the heat, stir in the mushrooms and turn into a 90 cl (1½ pint) pie dish.

To make the suetcrust, preheat the oven to 200°C (400°F or Mark 6). Sift the flour, baking powder, mustard and salt into a bowl. Coarsely grate the vegetable suet and add to the flour.

Mix in 12.5 to 15 cl (4 to 5 fl oz) of cold water to make a soft dough. Knead until just smooth.

Roll out the pastry on a floured surface until it is 2.5 cm (1 inch) larger than the top of the pie dish. Cut 1 cm (½ inch) wide strips from the edge of the pastry and press on to the dampened rim of the pie dish. Lift the large piece of pastry on top. Press together to seal, trim and crimp it. Make a hole in the centre.

Brush the pastry with skimmed milk, then decorate with trimmings and brush these also with the milk. Bake for 45 minutes. Serve hot.

Cornmeal Pancakes Filled with Chicken Picadillo

Serves 8

Working and
total time:
about 1 hour
and 15
minutes

Calories
190
Protein
14g
Cholesterol
20mg
Total fat
5g
Saturated fat
2g
Sodium
65mg

75 g	cornmeal	2½ oz	**1**	large garlic clove, crushed	1
60 g	plain flour	2 oz	**1 tbsp**	red wine vinegar	1 tbsp
1	egg	1	**1 tbsp**	mild chili powder	1 tbsp
30 cl	skimmed milk	½ pint	**2 tsp**	fresh oregano	2 tsp
2 tsp	corn oil	2 tsp	**½ tsp**	ground cumin	½ tsp
225 g	fromage frais	7½ oz		freshly ground black pepper	
3 tbsp	chopped fresh coriander	3 tbsp	**45 g**	raisins	1½ oz
1 tsp	safflower oil	1 tsp	**30 g**	stoned green olives, quartered	1 oz
	Chicken picadillo			flaked almonds	
500 g	tomatoes, skinned and chopped,	1 lb	**2 tsp**	capers, coarsely chopped	2 tsp
1	onion, finely chopped	1	**250 g**	cooked chicken, diced	8 oz

Combine the cornmeal and flour in a bowl and make a well in the centre. Break the egg into the well. Gradually beat the egg into the flour. As the mixture thickens, whisk in the milk. When it is all incorporated, whisk in the corn oil. Cover and set aside for 30 minutes.

Put the tomatoes, onion and garlic in a heavy saucepan and stir in the vinegar, chili powder, oregano, cumin and some pepper. Cook, covered, until the onion is soft and the sauce is quite thick—about 20 minutes. Stir occasionally.

Add the raisins, olives, almonds, capers and chicken, and stir. Cook until heated through.

Brush a little of the safflower oil over the base of a small frying pan. Stir the batter well, then pour 2 to 3 tablespoons at a time into the centre of the pan. Oil th pan after each pancake is cooked. Make eight.

Spoon a little of the picadillo on to the pancakes and roll them up. Top with the fromage frais. Sprinkle with the chopped coriander and serve hot.

Phyllo Triangles with Spinach and Feta Cheese

Serves 12

Working time:
about 1 hour
and 30
minutes

Total time:
about 2 hours

Calories
140
Protein
6g
Cholesterol
25mg
Total fat
8g
Saturated fat
3g
Sodium
155mg

12	sheets phyllo pastry, each 30 cm (12 inches) square	12
30 g	unsalted butter, melted	1 oz
3 tbsp	virgin olive oil	3 tbsp
	Spinach filling	
350 g	fresh spinach, chopped, washed	12 oz
1 tbsp	virgin olive oil	1 tbsp
1	large onion, finely chopped	1
1	garlic clove, finely chopped1	1
60 g	feta cheese, crumbled	2 oz

150 g	quark	5 oz
2 tbsp	chopped parsley	2 tbsp
1 tbsp	fresh oregano, chopped	1 tbsp
1½ tsp	fresh mint, chopped	1½ tsp
	freshly ground black pepper	
	Dill and feta cheese filling	
150 g	feta cheese	5 oz
150 g	silken tofu	5 oz
1	egg	1
3 tbsp	fresh dill, chopped	3 tbsp

Cook the spinach over medium heat in the water that clings to its leaves. Stir occasionally until it wilts—about 6 minutes. Drain well.

In a small sauté pan, heat the oil and cook the onion and the garlic, covered, over low heat until they are soft. Turn them into a bowl, add the spinach, feta, quark, parsley, oregano, mint and some pepper, and mix well.

Place the feta cheese in a bowl, mash, then mix in the tofu, egg, dill and some pepper.

Preheat the oven to 180°C (350°F or Mark 4).

To form the pastry triangles, stack up the sheets of phyllo and cut into four strips. Combine the melted butter with the oil and brush a little over one of the pastry strips.

Put a heaped teaspoon of one of the fillings at the bottom of the strip and fold one corner over to form a triangle. Press lightly, then fold again. Continue folding, making triangular pastry. Repeat to use up the rest of the fillings.

Lightly grease a baking sheet and brush the pastries with the oil and butter. Bake them until they are crisp and golden brown—15 to 20 minutes. Allow them to cool before serving.

Turkey Crust Pizza

Serves 8

Working time: about 30 minutes

Total time: about 1 hour and 30 minutes

Calories 290
Protein 32g
Cholesterol 75mg
Total fat 11g9
Saturated fat 4g
Sodium 460mg

1 kg	white and dark turkey meat, skinned, finely chopped	2 lb
45 g	dry breadcrumbs	1½ oz
1	spring onion, chopped	1
2	egg whites, lightly beaten	2
4 drops	Tabasco sauce	4 drops
2 tsp	virgin olive oil	2 tsp
¼ tsp	salt	¼ tsp
	freshly ground black pepper	
2 tbsp	white wine	2 tbsp
150 g	grated mozzarella and Gruyere cheese, combined	5 oz

	Pizza sauce	
1 tbsp	virgin olive oil	1 tbsp
90 g	onion, finely chopped	3 oz
1	green pepper, cut into strips	1
135 g	thinly sliced mushrooms	4½ oz
1 kg	canned whole plum tomatoes	35 oz
2	garlic cloves, finely chopped	2
2 tbsp	red wine vinegar	2 tbsp
2 tsp	sugar	2 tsp
1 tbsp	chopped fresh basil	1 tbsp
½ tsp	dried oregano	½ tsp
¼ tsp	salt	¼ tsp
	freshly ground black pepper	

Place the oil in a heavy saucepan over medium-low heat, and cook the onion for 3 minutes. Add the pepper strips and mushrooms and cook for 2 minutes. Add the rest of the sauce ingredients. Bring to the boil, reduce the heat and simmer for 40 minutes.

Preheat the oven to 200°C (400°F or Mark 6). Combine the breadcrumbs, spring onion, egg whites, Tabasco sauce, 1 teaspoon of the oil, and the salt and pepper in a large bowl. Add

12.5 cl (4 fl oz) of the sauce and the white wine. Mix in the turkey. Rub a shallow 25 to 30 cm (10 to 12 inch) round baking dish with the remaining oil. Spread the turkey mixture over the bottom of the dish pushing it up all round the sides to resemble a crust. Pour half of the warm sauce on to the turkey crust. Cover with the grated cheeses. Ladle on the remaining sauce. Sprinkle with black pepper. Bake for 15 minutes. Let stand for 5 minutes before serving.

Sage-Flavoured Chicken Pie with Phyllo Crust

Serves 4

Working time: about 1 hour

Total time: about 1 hour and 30 minutes

Calories 440
Protein 26g
Cholesterol 70mg
Total fat 17g
Saturated fat 6g
Sodium 370mg

350g	chicken breast, skinned, cubed	12 oz
1 tbsp	unsalted butter	1 tbsp
1	potato, peeled and cubed	1
1	onion, chopped	1
1	garlic clove, finely chopped	1
125g	mushrooms, quartered	4 oz
1	small carrot, diced	1
¼ tsp	salt	¼ tsp
	freshly ground black pepper	
1 tbsp	flour	1 tbsp

1 tbsp	chopped fresh sage	1 tbsp
1	small courgette, diced	1
½ litre	unsalted chicken stock	16 fl oz
2 tbsp	cornflour, (with 4 tbsp wine)	2 tbsp
	Phyllo crust	
125g	plain flour	4 oz
2 tbsp	virgin olive oil	2 tbsp
¼ tsp	salt	¼ tsp
3 tbsp	cornflour	3 tbsp
15g	unsalted butter	½ oz

Melt the butter in a large saucepan, add the potato, and cook, stirring, for 2 minutes. Add the onion, garlic, mushrooms, carrot, salt and pepper. Stir in the flour and mix well. Cook for 5 minutes. Add the sage, courgette and chicken. Cook until the courgette is soft.

Meanwhile, heat the chicken stock in a saucepan and reduce it to about 35 cl (12 fl oz). Whisk in the cornflour mixture and simmer until the sauce is thickened and shiny. Mix into the chicken mixture, and set aside.

Place the flour in a bowl and make a well in the centre. Pour in the oil and salt. Stir in water until a soft dough forms. On a board sprinkled with 1 tablespoon of the cornflour, knead the dough until elastic then roll into a thin circle.

Preheat the oven to 170°C (325°F or Mark 3). Melt the butter and brush half of it over the dough. Fit a round 25 cm (10 inch) baking dish at least 4 cm (1¼inches) deep over the dough. Cut the dough into a circle 1 cm (1½inch) larger then the pan all round.

Pour the filling into the ungreased baking dish and rest the dough on top. Brush with the remaining melted butter. Bake it until the surface tums golden—20 to 25 minutes.

Chicken Wrapped in Crisp Phyllo

Serves 6

Working time:
about 1 hour

Total time:
about 1 day

Calories
500

Protein
37g

Cholesterol
95mg

Total fat
27g

Saturated fat
7g

Sodium
545mg

6	chicken breasts, skinned	**6**
250 g	phyllo pastry (18 sheets)	**8 oz**
¾ tsp	salt	**¾ tsp**
¾ tsp	freshly ground black pepper	**¾ tsp**
4 tbsp	safflower oil	**4 tbsp**
1	garlic clove, finely chopped	**1**
1	shallot, finely chopped	**1**

350 g	fresh spinach, stemmed	**12 oz**
4 tbsp	dry white wine	**4 tbsp**
¼	unsalted chicken stock	**8 fl oz**
1 tbsp	double cream	**1 tbsp**
60 g	pistachio nuts, shelled, peeled and coarsely chopped	**2 oz**
250 g	low-fat ricotta cheese	**8 oz**

Slice each breast diagonally into three medallions. Sprinkle the pieces with ½ teaspoon each of the salt and pepper. Heat 1 tablespoon of the oil in a frying pan and sear the chicken for 30 seconds each side. Set aside.

Immediately add the garlic and shallot to the pan, and sauté for about 30 seconds, stirring. Add the spinach, reduce the heat, and cover. Cook until the spinach is wilted. Remove the pan from the heat and take out half of the spinach mixture. Chop finely and reserve.

Heat the pan again over medium heat. Pour in the wine and stock, and stir to deglaze the pan. Stir in the remaining salt and pepper and the cream, and cook until the liquid is reduced

by half. Purée the sauce in a blender. Pour it into a small saucepan and set it aside.

Preheat the oven to 170°C (325°F or Mark 3). For the filling, combine the pistachios, ricotta and chopped spinach. Unwrap the phyllo. Peel off a stack of three sheets about 30 by 45 cm (12 by 18 inches) and place on a dry work surface.

Centre a piece of chicken near an edge of the dough. Spread over a thin layer of filling, then top it with another piece, a second layer of filling and a third chicken slice. Fold the sides of the dough over and roll it up. Place the roll seam side down in an oiled baking dish. Make six rolls in all. Brush with the remaining oil.

Bake for 45 minutes. Serve on top of the sauce.

Chicken in a Tortilla Pie

Serves 4

Working time: about 20 minutes

Total time: about 30 minutes

Calories 550
Protein 54g
Cholesterol 170mg
Total fat 29g
Saturated fat 12g
Sodium 395mg

1.5 kg	chicken, wings removed, the rest skinned and quartered	**3 lb**
12.5 cl	unsalted chicken stock	**4 fl oz**
¼ tsp	ground coriander seeds	**¼ tsp**
⅛ tsp	cayenne pepper	**⅛ tsp**
¼ tsp	ground cumin	**¼ tsp**
1	green pepper, finely chopped	**1**
4	spring onions, finely chopped	**4**
¼ tsp	dried oregano	**¼ tsp**
1 tbsp	virgin olive oil	**1 tbsp**
	freshly ground black pepper	

175 g	cheddar cheese, grated	**6 oz**
2	(25 cm/10 inch) flour tortillas	**2**
⅛ tsp	chili powder	**⅛ tsp**
	Salsa	
2	ripe tomatoes, chopped	**2**
1 or 2	green chili peppers, chopped	**1 or 2**
2	garlic cloves, finely chopped	**2**
1	lime, juice only	**1**
1 tbsp	chopped coriander or parsley	**1 tbsp**
¼ tsp	salt	**¼ tsp**
	freshly ground black pepper	

Place the chicken pieces in a baking dish with the meatier part of each piece towards the edge. Pour in the stock, and sprinkle with the coriander, cayenne pepper and ⅛ teaspoon of the cumin. Cover with greaseproof paper and microwave on high for 10 minutes; turning after five minutes. Remove the breasts and microwave the leg quarters for 2 minutes more. Let the meat stand in the cooking liquid until it is cool. Discard the liquid and shred the meat.

Combine the green pepper, spring onions, oregano, oil, black pepper and the remaining cumin in a bowl. Cover with plastic film. Cook for 2 minutes on high, then remove from the oven and mix in the chicken.

In a separate bowl, mix the salsa ingredients. Add 12.5 cl (4 fl oz) of the salsa and half the cheese to the chicken. Place a tortilla on a plate, cover it with the chicken and put the other tortilla on top. Sprinkle with the remaining cheese and the chili powder. Microwave until the cheese melts. Cut into wedges and serve.

Swede Pancake

Serves 8

Working time:
about 25
minutes

Total time:
about 1 hour
and 15
minutes

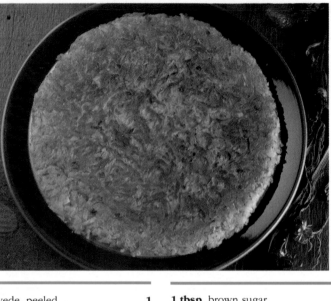

Calories
120
Protein
2g
Cholesterol
35mg
Total fat
6g
Saturated fat
1g
Sodium
155mg

1	small swede, peeled	1
2	medium potatoes, peeled	2
3	spring onions, thinly sliced	3
1 tbsp	cornflour, (with 1 tbsp water)	1 tbsp
1	whole egg, plus 1 egg white	1

1 tbsp	brown sugar	1 tbsp
½ tsp	salt	½ tsp
¼ tsp	cayenne pepper	¼ tsp
3 tbsp	safflower oil	3 tbsp

Coarsely grate the swede. Firmly squeeze the grated flesh, a handful at a time, over a sink to rid it of excess moisture; as you work, transfer the swede to a large bowl. Grate the potatoes into the bowl, then add the spring onions and stir well to combine the vegetables.

Whisk together the cornflour mixture and the eggs. Stir them into the vegetables with the brown sugar, salt and cayenne pepper. Mix well.

Heat 2 tablespoons of the oil in a large non-stick or well-seasoned Spanish omelette pan, or frying pan with removable handle, over medium-high heat. When the oil is hot, put the vegetable mixture in the pan and quickly flatten it with a spatula to a uniform thickness. Reduce the heat to medium low and cook the pancake until the bottom is golden-brown—20 to 25 minutes. To flip the pancake, first invert over the pancake a plate larger than the pan. Then turn the pan and plate over together, leaving the pancake on the plate. Preheat the oven to 190°C (375°F or Mark 5).

Heat the remaining tablespoon of oil in the pan over medium heat. Carefully slide the pancake from the plate back into the pan and cook it for 5 minutes. Then put the pan in the oven (removing the handle, if necessary) and bake the pancake until the bottom is golden-brown and the top crisp—about 25 minutes. Gently slide the pancake on to a serving plate, cut it into wedges and serve.

Leek Pie

Serves 6

Working time:
about 40
minutes

Total time:
about 1 hour

Calories
250
Protein
9g
Cholesterol
15mg
Total fat
8g
Saturated fat
3g
Sodium
145mg

1 kg	potatoes, peeled	2¼ lb
4 to 5 tbsp	skimmed milk	4 to 5 tbsp
75 g	Gruyère cheese, grated	2½ oz
	freshly ground black pepper	
750 g	leeks, washed thoroughly and trimmed	1½ lb
1	large onion, sliced	1

1 tbsp	virgin olive oil	1 tbsp
¼ tsp	salt	¼ tsp
2 tsp	mixed dried herbs	2 tsp
30 cl	unsalted chicken stock or skimmed milk	½ pint
15 g	unsalted butter	½ oz
15 g	plain flour	½ oz

Cut the potatoes into quarters, then steam them until cooked through—about 25 to 30 minutes. Mash the cooked potatoes well, beat in the milk and cheese and season with pepper. Put the potatoes into a large piping bag fitted with a large star nozzle and pipe an attractive border round the inside edge of a fireproof dish.

Cut the leeks into 1 cm (½ inch) thick slices. Heat the oil in a large shallow saucepan, then add the leeks, onion, salt and herbs. Cover the pan with a tightly fitting lid and cook gently until the leeks are just tender, shaking the pan frequently during cooking—25 to 30 minutes. Strain the juices from the leeks and make them up to 30 cl (½ pint) with chicken stock or milk. Set the leeks aside.

Melt the butter in the saucepan, add the flour, and stir in the leek juices and stock or milk. Bring to the boil, stirring all the time until the sauce thickens. Return the leeks to the pan, reduce the heat and simmer for 5 minutes.

Brown the piped potato border under a hot grill, then pour the leeks into the centre. Serve immediately.

Onion and Goat Cheese Pizza

Serves 8

Working time: about 40 minutes

Total time: about 2 hours and 30 minutes

Calories
220
Protein
6g
Cholesterol
10mg
Total fat
10g
Saturated fat
3g
Sodium
170mg

1.5 kg	onions, thinly sliced	**3 lb**
2 tbsp	virgin olive oil	**2 tbsp**
2 tsp	fresh thyme	**2 tsp**
6 cl	cider vinegar	**2 fl oz**
¼ tsp	salt	**¼ tsp**
1 tbsp	cornmeal	**1 tbsp**
90 g	mild goat cheese or feta cheese	**3 oz**
60 g	low-fat cream cheese	**2 oz**

Thyme-flavoured pizza dough

7 g	dried yeast	**¼ oz**
¼ tsp	sugar	**¼ tsp**
250 g	strong plain flour	**8 oz**
¼ tsp	salt	**¼ tsp**
2 tsp	fresh thyme	**2 tsp**
2 tbsp	virgin olive oil	**2 tbsp**

Pour 12.5 cl (4 fl oz) water into a bowl and add the yeast and sugar . Let stand for 2 to 3 minutes, then stir until the yeast and sugar are dissolved. Allow to stand in a warm place until it has doubled in bulk—about 15 minutes.

Sift 200 g (7 oz) of the flour and the salt into a bowl, and stir in the thyme. Make a well in the centre and pour in the yeast mixture and the oil. Knead until it is smooth and elastic.

Put the dough in a clean oiled bowl and cover it with a damp towel. Leave in a warm place until the dough has doubled in bulk.

Heat 1 tablespoon of the olive oil in a large casserole over medium heat. Cook the onions and thyme until the onions are well browned—

45 minutes to 1 hour. Add the vinegar and salt, and cook until the liquid has evaporated.

Preheat the oven to 230°C (450°F or Mark 8). Sprinkle the cornmeal on a large, heavy baking sheet. Form the dough into a circle about 20 cm (8 inches) in diameter. Place in the centre of the baking sheet and pat it out further.

Distribute the onions in an even layer over the pizza dough. Combine the goat or feta cheese and the cream cheese and add to the pizza. Bake for 10 minutes. Remove from the oven and dribble the remaining oil over the top. Return to the oven and bake until the crust is browned and the cheese turns golden. Cut the pizza into wedges and serve at once.

Devilled Mushroom Tartlets

Serves 8

Working time:
about 50
minutes

Total time:
about 1 hour
and 20
minutes

Calories
225
Protein
5g
Cholesterol
40mg
Total fat
15g
Saturated fat
5g
Sodium
130mg

600 g	small button mushrooms,	1¼ lb	15 g	plain flour	½ oz
1 tbsp	trimmed and wiped clean	1 tbsp	2 tbsp	finely cut chives	2 tbsp
1 tbsp	fresh lemon juice	1 tbsp	1 tbsp	chopped parsley	1 tbsp
¼ tsp	salt	¼ tsp		**Shortcrust pastry**	
	freshly ground black pepper		175 g	plain flour	6 oz
15 cl	soured cream	¼ pint	⅛ tsp	salt	⅛ tsp
1 tsp	prepared English mustard	1 tsp	90 g	polyunsaturated margarine	3 oz
⅛ tsp	cayenne pepper	⅛ tsp	1	large egg, beaten	1

Put the mushrooms, lemon juice, salt and some pepper into a saucepan. Cover and cook gently until the mushrooms are soft—10 to 15 minutes.

Drain the mushrooms in a colander set over a bowl. Pour the liquid back into the saucepan, bring to the boil, lower the heat and simmer until it is reduced by half—about 5 minutes.

Meanwhile, combine the soured cream, mustard, cayenne pepper and flour in a bowl, and whisk until smooth. Stir this cream into the mushroom juices and cook gently, until the sauce thickens. Stir in the mushrooms and the chives and remove from the heat. Cover the pan with plastic film and set aside.

Preheat the oven to 220°C (425°F or Mark 7). Sift the flour and salt into a bowl. Rub in the margarine. Reserve 1 teaspoon of the beaten egg and mix the rest with the dry ingredients and 2 teaspoons of water to make a dough.

Roll the pastry out thinly and cut out eight rounds large enough to fit 9.5 cm (3¾ inch) fluted tartlet tins. With the trimmings shape strips about 5 mm (¼ inch) wide. Fill the tins with the mushroom mixture and top with the moistened dough stips in a lattice pattern. Glaze with the beaten egg and bake until golden-brown—20 to 25 minutes. Serve hot, sprinkled with parsley.

Pears with a Spiced Walnut Crust

Serves 10

Working time:
about 40
minutes

Total time:
about 1 hour
and 20
minutes

Calories
285
Protein
3g
Cholesterol
6mg
Total fat
9g
Saturated fat
2g
Sodium
35mg

60 g	shelled walnuts	**2 oz**	**¼ tsp**	ground ginger	**¼ tsp**
150 g	plain flour	**5 oz**	**1**	lemon, grated rind only	**1**
6 tbsp	light brown sugar	**6 tbsp**	**½ tsp**	pure vanilla extract	**½ tsp**
30 g	unsalted butter	**1 oz**	**6**	pears	**6**
30 g	polyunsaturated margarine	**1 oz**	**300 g**	red currant jelly or apricot jam	**10 oz**
¼ tsp	ground mace	**¼ tsp**			

Preheat the oven to 190°C (375°F or Mark 5).

Spread the walnuts on a baking sheet and toast in the oven until their skins begin to pull away. Allow to cool to room temperature.

Put the toasted walnuts, flour, brown sugar, butter, margarine, mace, ginger and lemon rind into a blender. Process until the mixture resembles coarse meal. Sprinkle on the vanilla and 1 tablespoon of water, and process it in short bursts until it begins to hold together in dough pieces about 2.5 cm (1 inch) in diameter.

Rub the pieces between your fingers to finish blending the dough, then put the pieces into a 23 cm (9 inch) tart tin with a removable bottom. Spread out the dough, coating the bottom and sides of the tin with a very thin layer; crimp the top edge of the dough with your fingers. Put the tin into the refrigerator.

Peel, halve, and core the pears. Thinly slice each pear in half, then arrange 10 of the halves around the edge of the tart shell, pointing their narrow ends towards the centre. Flatten each half, slightly spreading out the slices. Arrange the two remaining halves in the centre.

Bake until the edges are browned and any juices rendered by the pears have evaporated—about 40 minutes. Set the tart aside to cool.

Cook the jelly or jam in a small saucepan over medium-low heat until it melts—about 4 minutes. If using jam, sieve it. Using a pastry brush, glaze the cooled pears with a thin coating of the melted jelly.

Apple and Pear Upside-Down Tartlets

Makes 6
tartlets

Working time:
about 35
minutes

Total time:
about 1 hour
and 10
minutes

Per tartlet:
Calories
210
Protein
3g
Cholesterol
0mg
Total fat
8g
Saturated fat
2g
Sodium
100mg

175 g	shortcrust dough (recipe, p 60) made with ¾ teaspoon of ground cinnamon added to dry ingredients	**6 oz**

2 tbsp	clear honey	**2 tbsp**
3	small dessert apples	**3**
3	small dessert pears	**3**
2 tsp	fresh lemon juice	**2 tsp**

Wrap the shortcrust dough in plastic film and chill it while making the filling.

Preheat the oven to 200°C (400°F or Mark 6). Lightly butter six 10 cm (4 inch) fluted tartlet tins. Boil the honey in a small saucepan for 1 minute. Pour a little hot honey into the buttered tins, evenly coating their bottoms. Peel, core and thinly slice the fruit, and toss the slices in the lemon juice to prevent discoloration. Arrange alternate layers of apples and pears in each tin, overlapping the slices in each layer. (Arrange the bottom layer of slices particularly carefully; this will be the top when the tartlets are inverted.) The layered fruit should rise slightly above the top of the tin.

Cut the dough into six equal pieces and roll out each piece on a lightly floured surface into a circle a little wider than the top of a tartlet tin. Neaten the edges, then place the dough circles over the fruit, tucking their edges inside the tins. Seal the dough to the fluted rims of the tins by pressing with your fingers all round the inside edges.

Bake the tartlets until the pastry is golden-brown—25 to 30 minutes. Leave them in their tins for a few minutes, then invert them on to serving plates. Serve the tartlets warm or cold.

Editor's Notes: A little extra honey can be dribbled over the top of the tartlets for serving.

Shortcrust Dough

Makes
about 275 g
(9 oz)

Working
(and total)
time: about
10 minutes

| **175 g** | plain flour | **6 oz** | **90 g** | polyunsaturated margarine | **3 oz** |
| **1 tsp** | sugar | **1 tsp** | **1** | egg white, lightly beaten | **1** |

Sift the flour and sugar into a mixing bowl. Add the margarine and rub it into the dry ingredients with your fingertips until the mixture resembles fine breadcrumbs. Add the egg white and mix it in with a roundbladed knife to form a dough. Gather the dough into a firm ball and knead it briefly on a lightly floured surface until smooth; do not overwork the dough or it will become oily and the baked pastry will be tough. Roll out the dough as required.

Editor's Notes: Shortcrust dough may be stored, wrapped in plastic film, in the refrigerator for up to a week or in the freezer for up to three months.

Souffléed Coffee Diamonds

Makes 10 diamonds

Working time: about 40 minutes

Total time: about 3 hours (includes chilling)

Per diamond:
Calories
170
Protein
3g
Cholesterol
30mg
Total fat
11g
Saturated fat
4g
Sodium
100mg

175 g	plain flour	**6 oz**
90 g	polyunsaturated margarine, chilled	**3 oz**
2 tbsp	dark brown sugar	**2 tbsp**
¼ tbsp	cocoa powder	**¼ tbsp**

	Coffee soufflé	
1	egg yolk	**1**
45 g	light brown sugar	**1½ oz**
3 tbsp	strong black coffee	**3 tbsp**
1 tsp	powdered gelatine	**1 tsp**
2	egg whites	**2**
8 cl	whipping cream	**3 fl oz**

Sift the flour into a bowl. Rub in the margarine until the mixture resembles fine breadcrumbs, then stir in the sugar. Add 2 teaspoons of water and mix to a firm dough. Gather into a ball and knead it on a floured surface until smooth.

Roll out the dough to a thickness of 3 mm (⅛ inch) and cut out ten diamonds. Use these to line smaller diamond-shaped tartlet tins. Prick with a fork, put them on a baking sheet and chill for 30 minutes. Cut out 30 small leaves from the trimmings and chill also. Preheat the oven to 220°C (425°F or Mark 7).

Bake the leaves for about 3 minutes and the diamond cases for 15 to 20 minutes, until crisp and lightly browned. Allow to cool.

To make the soufflé, whisk the egg yolk, sugar and coffee in a bowl until pale and frothy. Sprinkle the gelatine over 2 tablespoons of water in a bowl, leave to soften, then place over a saucepan of simmering water, and stir until the gelatine has completely dissolved. Pour it into the coffee mixture, beating well.

Chill the mixture until it has almost set—about 30 minutes. Whisk the two egg whites until stiff, and whip the cream until stiff. Fold the cream, then the egg whites, into the coffee mixture. Chill again until lightly set.

Pipe swirls of the soufflé into the cases. Sprinkle with cocoa powder and decorate with the leaves. Chill for 30 minutes before serving.

Almond and Persimmon Stars

1	sheet phyllo pastry, about 45 by 30 cm (18 by 12 inches)	1
2 tbsp	ground amaretti biscuits	2 tbsp
30 g	margarine, melted	1 oz

2	persimmons, peeled, one chopped, one sliced	2
3 tbsp	ground almonds	3 tbsp
1	egg white	1

Grease and lightly flour twelve 7.5 cm (3 inch) shallow, flat-based tartlet tins. Preheat the oven to 200°C (400°F or Mark 6).

Spread the phyllo out on a work surface and brush it with the melted margarine. Cut the sheet into twenty-four 7.5 cm (3 inch) squares. Line each tartlet tin with two squares of phyllo, arranging the corners to form an eight-pointed star.

To make the filling, purée the chopped persimmon in a blender or food processor. Transfer the purée to a mixing bowl and stir in the ground almonds and amaretti biscuit crumbs. In a separate bowl, whisk the egg white until it is stiff, then fold it gently into the persimmon-amaretti mixture.

Distribute the filling among the phyllo stars and bake them until the pastry is golden—15 to 20 minutes. Allow the stars to cool briefly in their tins, then unmould them on to wire racks to cool completely.

Decorate each star with the slices of persimmon. Serve the stars on the day they are baked, while the pastry is still crisp.

Phyllo Fruit Squares

Makes 10 squares

Working time: about 30 minutes

Total time: about 1 hour and 25 minutes

Per square:
Calories 135
Protein 6g
Cholesterol trace
Total fat 3g
Saturated fat 2g
Sodium 25mg

30 g	unsalted butter, melted	**1 oz**
1	large orange, rind grated, peel and pith removed, cut into segments	**1**
1 tbsp	caster sugar	**1 tbsp**
90 g	raisins	**3 oz**
90 g	sultanas	**3 oz**

1	cooking apple, peeled and grated	**1**
10	sheets phyllo pastry, each about 45 by 30cm (18 by 12 inches)	**10**
3 tsp	clear honey	**3 tsp**
1 tbsp	flaked almonds	**1 tbsp**
2 tsp	orange-flower water	**2 tsp**

Preheat the oven to 190°C (375°F or Mark 5). Brush a 28 by 18 by 4 cm (11 by 7 by 1½ inch) baking tin with a little of the melted butter.

Chop the orange segments and add them to the bowl with the raisins, sultanas, apple and 2 teaspoons of the orange rind. Mix well.

Keep the sheets of phyllo covered by a clean, damp cloth, removing them as required. Lay one sheet in the prepared tin so that it overhangs all four sides. Brush with melted butter and cover with another sheet. Brush this with butter and cover with a third. Sprinkle one third of the fruit mixture over the phyllo in the tin and dribble on 1 teaspoon of the honey. Fold over the four overhanging edges, one after another, and brush these edges with butter.

Repeat the above procedure to make two more layers of phyllo and filling. Lay the final sheet of phyllo over the top, neatly folding the four edges underneath. Brush the top with butter and lightly mark it into a lattice design with a knife. Sprinkle over the almonds.

Bake in the oven until golden-brown—25 to 30 minutes. Towards the end of the baking time, prepare a syrup. Heat the sugar and orange-flower water in a saucepan with 2 tablespoons of water. Stir the mixture until the sugar has dissolved, then boil it for 1 minute.

Remove the baked phyllo fruit pastry from the oven and pour the syrup over the top. Allow to cool before cutting into squares and serving.

Cherry Triangles

Makes 12 triangles		
Working time: about 40 minutes		
Total time: about 1 hour and 20 minutes		

	Per triangle:
	Calories 90
	Protein 2g
	Cholesterol 0mg
	Total fat 6g
	Saturated fat trace
	Sodium 25mg

125 g	fromage frais	**4 oz**
15 g	caster sugar	**¼ oz**
1 tbsp	kirsch	**1 tbsp**
500 g	cherries, stoned	**1 lb**

8	sheets phyllo pastry, each about 45 by 30 cm (18 by 12 inches)	**8**
3 tsp	safflower oil	**3 tsp**
	icing sugar, to decorate	

Preheat the oven to 200°C (400°F or Mark 6).

To make the filling, place the *fromage frais*, caster sugar and kirsch in a mixing bowl. Reserve 12 cherries for decoration. Quarter the remainder and gently fold them into the *fromage frais* mixture. Keep the sheets of phyllo covered by a clean, damp cloth to prevent them from drying out, removing them as needed.

Lay one sheet of phyllo on a work surface. Brush it lightly with oil and cover it with a second sheet. Cut this double sheet lengthwise into three strips, each 10 cm (4 inches) wide. Place one tablespoon of filling at one end of a strip, then fold a corner of the phyllo over the filling to form a neat triangle. Continue folding over the filled triangle until you reach the end of the strip, keeping the shape as you work. Tuck in the loose end and transfer the triangular parcel—seam down—to a lightly oiled baking sheet. Make up the two remaining strips in the same way, then make another nine triangles with the remaining phyllo and filling.

Brush the phyllo triangles with the remaining oil and bake them until they are crisp and golden—9 to 10 minutes. Transfer them to a wire rack to cool.

Before serving, halve the remaining cherries. Sift a little icing sugar over the top of each triangle and serve with the cherries.

Apple Slice

Serves 8

Working time: about 45 minutes

Total time: about 2 hours and 20 minutes

Calories 260

Protein 3g

Cholesterol 0mg

Total fat 11g

Saturated fat 2g

Sodium 100mg

150 g	wholemeal flour	**5 oz**
1 tsp	light brown sugar	**1 tsp**
90 g	polyunsaturated margarine	**3 oz**
30 g	shelled hazelnuts, toasted, skinned and ground	**1 oz**
1	egg white	**1**
1 tbsp	apricot jam, no added sugar	**1 tbsp**

	Apple-lime filling	
1 kg	cooking apples, peeled, cored and sliced	**2 lb**
1	lime, grated rind and juice	**1**
90 g	caster sugar	**3 oz**
2	dessert apples	**2**
2 tsp	icing sugar	**2 tsp**

Lightly butter a 35 by 11 cm (14 by 4½ inch) loose-based fluted or plain tart tin.

Sift the flour and sugar into a bowl. Rub in the margarine until the mixture resembles fine breadcrumbs. With a round bladed knife, blend in the ground hazelnuts and the egg white. Knead the dough briefly on a floured surface until it is smooth, then roll it out into a rectangle 2.5 cm (1 inch) larger all round than the tart tin. Lift the dough with the rolling pin and ease it into the tin, pressing it into the fluted edges. Trim off excess and prick the inside with a fork. Chill while preparing the filling.

Preheat the oven to 190°C (375°F or Mark 5). To make the filling, place the cooking apples in a large saucepan with the grated lime rind, half the lime juice and 2 tablespoons of water. Cover, bring to the boil, then cook gently until the apples are tender. Stir in the caster sugar and boil off any excess, then set the pan aside. Peel, core and thinly slice the dessert apples. Toss the slices in the remaining lime juice.

Spread the apple mixture in the dough case and lay on overlapping apple slices. Sift on the icing sugar. Bake the tart in the oven until the pastry is golden-brown—30 to 40 minutes.

In a small pan set over gentle heat, warm the apricot jam with a tablespoon of water. Sieve, then use a pastry brush to glaze over the apple slices. Allow to cool, slice and serve.

Fig Flowers

Makes 16 flowers

Working time: about 40 minutes

Total time: about 1 hour and 20 minutes

Per flower:
Calories 105
Protein 2g
Cholesterol 0mg
Total fat 7g
Saturated fat 1g
Sodium 80mg

150 g	plain flour	**5 oz**
30 g	cornmeal	**1 oz**
1 tsp	caster sugar	**1 tsp**
90 g	polyunsaturated margarine	**3 oz**
1	egg white	**1**

	Creamy fig filling	
5	ripe figs, quartered lengthwise	**5**
125 g	medium-fat soft cheese	**4 oz**
1 tbsp	plain low-fat yogurt	**1 tbsp**
1 tsp	rose-water	**1 tsp**
1 tsp	sugar	**1 tsp**

To make the dough, sift the flour, cornmeal and sugar into a mixing bowl, then rub in the margarine with your fingertips until the mixture resembles fine breadcrumbs Mix in the egg white with a round-bladed knife, then gather the dough into a ball and knead it briefly on a lightly floured surface until smooth.

Roll the dough out to a thickness of about 3 mm ($\frac{1}{8}$ inch) and cut out 16 shapes with a 7.5 cm (3 inch) flower cutter. Fit the shapes into 7. 5 cm (3 inch) tartlet tins, easing the dough across the base and up the sides of the tins without spoiling the petals. Prick the insides with a fork and chill the flower-shaped

cases for 30 minutes. Meanwhile, preheat the oven to 190°C (375°F or Mark 5).

Bake the tartlet cases until they are lightly browned at the edges—7 to 10 minutes. Allow them to cool.

To fill the tartlets, cut the fig quarters lengthwise into thin slices, and arrange the slices in the pastry flowers to look like petals. Using a wooden spoon, mix together the soft cheese, yogurt, rose-water and sugar until the mixture becomes smooth and creamy. Transfer the cheese mixture to a piping bag fitted with a 5 mm ($\frac{1}{4}$ inch) star nozzle and pipe a mound of filling into the centre of each fig flower.

Apple Streusel Slices

Serves 20

Working time:
about 40
minutes

Total time:
about 2 hours

Calories
135
Protein
2g
Cholesterol
0mg
Total fat
5g
Saturated fat
1g
Sodium
55mg

100 g	polyunsaturated margarine	**3½ oz**		**Sesame streusel**	
200 g	wholemeal flour	**7 oz**	**30 g**	polyunsaturated margarine	**1 oz**
750 g	dessert apples, peeled, cored and chopped	**1½ lb**	**75 g**	wholemeal flour	**2½ oz**
			30 g	demerara sugar	**1 oz**
60 g	dark brown sugar	**2 oz**	**1½ tbsp**	sesame seeds	**1½ tbsp**
2 tsp	ground cinnamon	**2 tsp**	**1 tsp**	ground cinnamon	**1 tsp**
90 g	sultanas	**3 oz**			

Rub the margarine into the flour in a bowl until the mixture resembles breadcrumbs Stir in about 3 tablespoons of iced water—enough to make a fairly firm dough—and knead lightly until the dough is smooth. Wrap the dough in plastic film and leave it to rest for 10 minutes.

Roll the dough out thinly on a lightly floured surface, and use it to line a 30 by 20 cm (12 by 8 inch) Swiss roll tin. Prick the dough with a fork and refrigerate it for about 15 minutes.

Meanwhile, preheat the oven to 200°C (400°F or Mark 6). Put the chopped apples in

a bowl, with the sugar, cinnamon and sultanas, and mix them together.

To make the sesame streusel, rub the margarine into the flour in a bowl until the mixture resembles breadcrumbs. Stir in the sugar, sesame seeds and cinnamon. Sprinkle 3 tablespoons of the mixture over the dough in the tin to absorb the juice from the apples. Spread the apple mixture in the tin. Sprinkle the remaining streusel over the apples. Bake the cake for 30 to 35 minutes, until the streusel is golden-brown. Cut into slices when cool.

Redcurrant Meringue Squares

Makes 24
squares

Working time:
about 40
minutes

Total time
about 4 hours
and 30
minutes

Per square:
Calories
90
Protein
1g
Cholesterol
0mg
Total fat
3g
Saturated fat
1g
Sodium
40mg

275 g	shortcrust dough	9 oz
750 g	redcurrants, picked over	1½ lb
175 g	caster sugar	6 oz

| 1 tbsp | cornflour | 1 tbsp |
| 2 | egg whites | 2 |

Roll the dough out into a rectangle on a lightly floured surface and trim it to line the base of a 30 by 20 cm (12 by 8 inch) baking tin. Lift the dough on a rolling pin and ease it into the tin, pressing it down gently. Prick the dough with a fork and chill it for 30 minutes. Meanwhile, preheat the oven to 220°C (425°F or Mark 7).

Bake the pastry for 20 to 25 minutes, until lightly browned, then remove it from the oven and reduce the oven temperature to 70°C (160°F or Mark ¼).

Put the redcurrants with 90 g (3 oz) of the sugar in a non-reactive saucepan. Cook over a low heat until the berries are soft and the mixture is liquid—4 to 5 minutes. Blend the

cornflour with 1 tablespoon of water, stirring to form a smooth paste. Add the cornflour paste to the redcurrants, bring to the boil and cook, stirring, until the mixture thickens and clears—about 2 minutes. Spread the redcurrant mixture over the cooked pastry base.

Whisk the egg whites until they form peaks, then gradually whisk in the remaining sugar until the mixture is stiff and glossy. Transfer the mixture to a piping bag fitted with an 8 mm (⅓ inch) star nozzle, and pipe a diagonal lattice pattern over the redcurrants. Bake the tart for 2 hours, then turn off the heat and allow the tart to cool inside the oven. Cut into twenty-four 5 cm (2 inch) squares for serving.

Plum Pizza

Serves 10

Working time:
about 45
minutes

Total time:
about 2 hours
and 30
minutes

Calories
240
Protein
7g
Cholesterol
105mg
Total fat
8g
Saturated fat
3g
Sodium
35mg

30 g	skimmed milk powder	**1 oz**
90 g	medium-fat curd cheese	**3 oz**
90 g	thick Greek yogurt	**3 oz**
2 tbsp	clear honey	**2 tbsp**
1 tsp	ground cinnamon	**1 tsp**
750 g	red plums, stoned and quartered	**1½ lb**
2 tbsp	apricot jam without added sugar	**2 tbsp**

Yeast dough

15 g	fresh yeast	**½ oz**
6 tbsp	milk, tepid	**6 tbsp**
30 g	caster sugar	**1 oz**
250 g	strong plain flour	**8 oz**
⅛ tsp	salt	**⅛ tsp**
30 g	unsalted butter, melted	**1 oz**
1	egg, beaten	**1**

To make the dough, mix the yeast with the milk, the sugar and 1 tablespoon of the flour. Leave the liquid in a warm place for 10 to 15 minutes to froth. Then mix the liquid with the salt, butter, egg and remaining flour, and knead the dough on a lightly floured surface for 5 minutes. Put the dough in an oiled bowl, cover it with oiled plastic film and leave it to rise for about 1 hour, until doubled in volume.

Meanwhile, preheat the oven to 200°C (400°F or Mark 6). Beat the milk powder, curd cheese, yogurt, honey and cinnamon together

with a wooden spoon and set aside. Grease a 25 cm (10 inch) sandwich tin.

On a lightly floured surface, roll out the risen dough to approximately the size of the tin. Press the dough against the tin's base and sides. Spread the cheese mixture over the dough and arrange the plums on the top, cut side down. Bake the pizza for about 30 minutes, until the dough is golden-brown and the plums are tender.

Leave the pizza to cool for 15 minutes, then warm the jam in a small saucepan and brush it over the plums. Serve the pizza just warm.

Glazed Fruit Tartlets

Makes 16 tartlets

Working time: about 1 hour

Total time: about 1 hour and 30 minutes

Per tartlet:
Calories 120
Protein 3g
Cholesterol 5mg
Total fat 4g
Saturated fat 2g
Sodium 110mg

140 g	sifted plain flour	**5 oz**
30 g	cold unsalted butter	**1 oz**
15 g	polyunsaturated margarine	**½ oz**
½ tsp	salt	**½ tsp**
2 tbsp	caster sugar	**2 tbsp**
½ tsp	pure vanilla extract	**½ tsp**
2	ripe nectarines	**2**

300 g	redcurrant jelly or apricot jam	**10 oz**
125 g	fresh raspberries	**4 oz**
	Cream filling	
175 g	low-fat cottage cheese	**6 oz**
1	lemon, grated rind only	**1**
2 tbsp	caster sugar	**2 tbsp**

Preheat the oven to 200°C (400°F or Mark 6).

Put the flour, butter, margarine, salt and sugar into a food processor and blend just long enough to produce a fine-meal texture. Add the vanilla extract and 2 tablespoons of water, and continue blending until the mixture forms a ball. Shape into a log about 20 cm (8 inches) long, then wrap it in plastic film, and chill.

For the filling, purée the cottage cheese in a blender so that the curd is no longer visible, then blend in the lemon rind and the 2 tablespoons of sugar. Refrigerate the filling.

To form the tartlet shells, divide the dough into 16 equal pieces. Press each piece of dough into a fluted or round tartlet tin. Freeze the

tartlet shells for 10 minutes. Set the shells on a baking sheet and bake them until their edges start to brown—6 to 8 minutes. Leave the tartlet shells in their tins to cool to room temperature.

Halve the nectarines lengthwise, discarding the stones, then thinly slice the halves. Melt the jelly or jam in a small saucepan over medium heat, stirring often. If using jam, sieve it. Allow the mixture to cool slightly.

Remove the tartlet shells from the tins, then spread about 2 teaspoons of the chilled filling inside each shell. Arrange the nectarine slices and raspberries on top. Brush the fruit lightly with the jelly. If the jelly cools, reheat it, stirring constantly, until it is thin enough to spread.

Gingery Peach and Almond Tartlets

Serves 10

Working time:
about 45
minutes

Total time:
about 1 hour
and 30
minutes

Calories
150
Protein
3g
Cholesterol
60mg
Total fat
6g
Saturated fat
1g
Sodium
35mg

5	firm but ripe peaches	**5**	**½ tsp**	finely chopped fresh ginger root	**½ tsp**
75 g	blanched almonds	**2½ oz**	**100 g**	caster sugar	**3½ oz**
4 tbsp	plain flour	**4 tbsp**	**2**	eggs	**2**
½ tsp	baking powder	**½ tsp**	**15 g**	unsalted butter, softened	**½ oz**

Blanch the peaches in boiling water until their skins loosen—30 seconds to 1 minute. Peel, then cut them in half, discarding the stones.

Preheat the oven to 170°C (325°F or Mark 3).

Put the almonds, flour, baking powder, ginger and sugar into a blender; blend the mixture until the nuts are very finely chopped. Add the eggs and butter, and process them just long enough to blend them in.

Slice one of the peach halves lengthwise and arrange the slices in a lightly oiled 10 cm (4 inch) tartlet tin. Cut and arrange the remaining peach halves the same way. Spoon the almond mixture over the peaches and bake the tartlets until they are lightly browned—30 to 40 minutes.

Let the tartlets cool on a wire rack, then remove them from the tins and serve.

Useful weights and measures

Weight Equivalents

Avoirdupois		Metric
1 ounce	=	28.35 grams
1 pound	=	254.6 grams
2.3 pounds	=	1 kilogram

Liquid Measurements

$^1/_4$ pint	=	$1^1/_2$ decilitres
$^1/_2$ pint	=	$^1/_4$ litre
scant 1 pint	=	$^1/_2$ litre
$1^3/_4$ pints	=	1 litre
1 gallon	=	4.5 litres

Liquid Measures

1 pint	=	20 fl oz	=	32 tablespoons
$^1/_2$ pint	=	10 fl oz	=	16 tablespoons
$^1/_4$ pint	=	5 fl oz	=	8 tablespoons
$^1/_8$ pint	=	$2^1/_2$ fl oz	=	4 tablespoons
$^1/_{16}$ pint	=	$1^1/_4$ fl oz	=	2 tablespoons

Solid Measures

1 oz almonds, ground = $3^3/_4$ level tablespoons
1 oz breadcrumbs fresh = 7 level tablespoons
1 oz butter, lard = 2 level tablespoons
1 oz cheese, grated = $3^1/_2$ level tablespoons
1 oz cocoa = $2^3/_4$ level tablespoons
1 oz desiccated coconut = $4^1/_2$ tablespoons
1 oz cornflour = $2^1/_2$ tablespoons
1 oz custard powder = $2^1/_2$ tablespoons
1 oz curry powder and spices = 5 tablespoons
1 oz flour = 2 level tablespoons
1 oz rice, uncooked = $1^1/_2$ tablespoons
1 oz sugar, caster and granulated = 2 tablespoons
1 oz icing sugar = $2^1/_2$ tablespoons
1 oz yeast, granulated = 1 level tablespoon

American Measures

16 fl oz	=1 American pint
8 fl oz	=1 American standard cup
0.50 fl oz	=1 American tablespoon

(slightly smaller than British Standards Institute tablespoon)

0.16 fl oz	=1 American teaspoon

Australian Cup Measures
(Using the 8-liquid-ounce cup measure)

1 cup flour	4 oz
1 cup sugar (crystal or caster)	8 oz
1 cup icing sugar (free from lumps)	5 oz
1 cup shortening (butter, margarine)	8 oz
1 cup brown sugar (lightly packed)	4 oz
1 cup soft breadcrumbs	2 oz
1 cup dry breadcrumbs	3 oz
1 cup rice (uncooked)	6 oz
1 cup rice (cooked)	5 oz
1 cup mixed fruit	4 oz
1 cup grated cheese	4 oz
1 cup nuts (chopped)	4 oz
1 cup coconut	$2^1/_2$ oz

Australian Spoon Measures

	level tablespoon
1 oz flour	2
1 oz sugar	$1^1/_2$
1 oz icing sugar	2
1 oz shortening	1
1 oz honey	1
1 oz gelatine	2
1 oz cocoa	3
1 oz cornflour	$2^1/_2$
1 oz custard powder	$2^1/_2$

Australian Liquid Measures
(Using 8-liquid-ounce cup)

1 cup liquid	8 oz
$2^1/_2$ cups liquid	20 oz (1 pint)
2 tablespoons liquid	1 oz
1 gill liquid	5 oz ($^1/_4$ pint)